EVERYDAY LIFE IN

The Renaissance

MARSHALL CAVENDISH
BENCHMARK
NEW YORK

KATHRYN HINDS

THE AUTHOR AND PUBLISHERS WOULD LIKE TO THANK MONICA CHOJNACKA, ASSOCIATE PROFESSOR OF HISTORY, UNIVERSITY OF GEORGIA, FOR HER GENEROUS ASSISTANCE IN READING THE MANUSCRIPT.

MARSHALL CAVENDISH BENCHMARK 99 WHITE PLAINS ROAD TARRYTOWN, NEW YORK 10591 www.marshallcavendish.us Text copyright © 2010 by Marshall Cavendish Corporation All rights reserved. No part of this book may be reproduced or utilized in any form or by any means electronic or mechanical including photocopying, recording, or by any information storage and retrieval system, without permission from the copyright holders. All Internet sites were available and accurate when this book was sent to press. LIBRARY OF CONGRESS CATALOGING-IN-PUBLICATION DATA Hinds, Kathryn, 1962– Everyday life in the Renaissance / by Kathryn Hinds. p. cm. Summary: "Describes the social and economic structure of life in the Renaissance (from roughly 1400–1600), including the ruling classes, the peasantry, the urban dwellers, and members of the Church and the role each group played in shaping European civilization"—Provided by publisher. ISBN 978-0-7614-4483-1 1. Renaissance—Juvenile literature. 2. Europe—Civilization—Juvenile literature. I. Title. CB361.H563 2010 940.2'1—dc22 2008054829

EDITOR: JOYCE STANTON PUBLISHER: MICHELLE BISSON
ART DIRECTOR: ANAHID HAMPARIAN SERIES DESIGNER: PATRICE SHERIDAN

Printed in Malaysia
135642

Front cover: The lady and the lute player were painted in the sixteenth century by a Venetian artist whose name has been lost to us.

Title page: A country scene by Pieter Brueghel the Younger, a Flemish artist who lived from around 1564 to 1638

Back cover: Sofonisba Anguissola, a famous Renaissance artist, painted this picture of her three sisters and a maid enjoying a game of chess outdoors.

Contents

About the Renaissance

WHEN WE TALK ABOUT THE RENAISSANCE, we generally mean the period of western European history from roughly 1400 to 1600. The Renaissance can also be understood as a cultural movement, in which art, literature, music, philosophy, and education shared in certain trends and influences. This movement had its origins in fourteenth-century Florence, Italy. Here the great writer Francesco Petrarca, or Petrarch, promoted the rebirth of the literature and learning of ancient Greece and Rome—*renaissance* means "rebirth."

Petrarch's ideas gradually spread through Italy and much of the rest of western Europe. People also grew interested in giving new life to Greek and

Above: The Renaissance produced some of the world's greatest artists. This angel playing music is the work of Venetian artist Giovanni Bellini.

Roman styles of art and architecture. In the process of rediscovering ancient culture and adapting it to the times, Renaissance people began to create unique cultures of their own. Many Europeans developed a great love of art and learning for their own sake.

Some Renaissance thinkers felt that they were living at the dawn of a magnificent new era, leaving behind a time they considered the "dark ages." They believed that they would not only revive the glories of the ancient world but surpass them. This belief seemed to be confirmed as new artistic techniques, architectural styles, philosophies, and educational practices caught on all over Europe. Historians now realize, however, that the seeds of these achievements were already present in medieval Europe. Although the Renaissance did not make a total break with the past, three momentous changes occurred during this period that definitely paved the way to the future.

First was the invention of movable type and the printing press. Two German goldsmiths, Johannes Gutenberg and Johann Fust, invented movable type in 1446–1448. Between 1450 and 1455 Gutenberg used the world's first printing press to produce the world's first printed book, the famous Gutenberg Bible. Before this, books had been written out and produced entirely by hand. They were therefore expensive and fairly rare. Since most people could not afford to own books, most people did not learn how to read. With the printing press, books—and the ideas and stories contained in them—became much more widely available.

Above: A portrait of a lady, by the famous artist, sculptor, architect, and engineer Leonardo da Vinci

Second, the Renaissance was a period when Europeans made many voyages of exploration. Explorers originally sought new routes to Asia, the source of silk, spices, and other goods that brought high prices in European markets. In 1492 the Italian explorer Christopher Columbus landed on the island of Hispaniola in the Caribbean. At first people thought that this land was part of Asia. By 1500, though, it was clear that Columbus had reached a continent whose existence had been previously unknown to most Europeans. This was a true turning point in world history.

The third great change was the Protestant Reformation. For more than a thousand years, most western Europeans had belonged to a single, unified

Above: Two well-dressed sisters sit beside their brother and the family dog, in this painting by Italian artist Sofonisba Anguissola.

Church, headquartered in the ancient Italian city of Rome. Then, in 1517, a monk named Martin Luther nailed a list of protests to a German cathedral door. Luther hoped to reform the Church, to purify it and rid it of corrupt practices. Instead, his action sparked the beginning of a new religious movement. Soon there were many conflicting ideas about what it meant to be a Christian. As new churches were founded, nations and individuals struggled to find their place in a changing world.

Renaissance people had many of the same joys and sorrows, hopes and fears that we do. They were poised at the beginning of the modern age, but still their world was very different from ours. Forget about cell phones, computers, cars, and televisions, and step back into a time when printed books were a wonderful new thing. Let the Renaissance come alive. . . .

The Court

One

A VARIETY OF COURTS

I f you were to look at a map of Europe during the Renaissance, you probably would be surprised. Its borders would appear very different from the way they do today. Many nations that exist now were then just taking shape, or were divided into a number of independent states. Governments also took various forms, but all were dominated by people in the highest levels of society. Leaders came from ancient noble families or, in many cities, from wealthy merchant families. Most Renaissance states were headed by a single person—a nobleman, king, or, in a few cases, queen. To get a full picture of life at the courts of such rulers, it is helpful to first take a look at the world in which they ruled.

ON THE ITALIAN PENINSULA

Italy is considered the birthplace of the Renaissance. Yet Italy was not a unified nation during this period. Instead, the Italian peninsula was occupied

Giorgio Vasari—painter, architect, and art historian—decorated a palace wall with this portrait of Cosimo de' Medici, the unofficial ruler of Florence, surrounded by artists and philosophers. Like many Renaissance rulers and nobles, members of the Medici family used their wealth and influence to support learning and the arts.

by about 250 independent or semi-independent states. Most of these were city-states, in which one city not only governed itself but also ruled the surrounding region. Many city-states were quite small, but a few controlled considerable territory, including other cities as well as rural areas.

A large portion of northern Italy was part of the Holy Roman Empire. The empire was based in Austria, however, and the emperor usually left his Italian lands alone. City-states that were within the boundaries of the Holy Roman Empire were generally free to govern themselves. Much of central Italy was ruled by the pope, head of the Catholic Church. The area under his authority was called the Papal States, and its heart was the city of Rome. Some cities in the Papal States were basically independent, but in much of the area the pope had absolute control. Southern Italy belonged to the Kingdom of Naples, which was under Spanish rule for most of the Renaissance.

Many Italian city-states were republics, governed by committees of elected representatives. A number of the largest and most influential city-states, though, were ruled by a single nobleman, usually with the title of marquis or duke. When he died, his title and position passed to his oldest son or, if there was no son, to a brother or nephew.

The city-state of Florence began the Renaissance as a republic and ended it as a dukedom. In the beginning, eight hundred wealthy families made up the city's ruling class, but by the 1430s one family had come to dominate all the others. This was the Medici, who ran the largest bank in Europe. At first they exercised their power behind the scenes, then they more openly took charge of the government of Florence. Finally in the 1530s the Medici were recognized as hereditary dukes of Florence.

THE HOLY ROMAN EMPIRE

Nearly the whole German-speaking area of Europe was officially part of the Holy Roman Empire. The emperor was elected by a group of German noblemen. Beginning in 1438 the nobles always elected a member of the powerful royal family of the Habsburgs. The Habsburgs, especially Maximilian I, made the most of the grandeur and symbolic importance of being emperor, and the family became even stronger. Through a combination of warfare and marriages, the Habsburg influence eventually extended from Spain to Hungary.

In spite of the large amount of territory under the Holy Roman Emperors' control, they generally concentrated their attention on their domains in Austria and eastern Europe. The area that is now Germany was a jigsaw puzzle of more or less independent states. Some were ruled by hereditary princes, counts, or dukes. Others were basically city-states governed by elected mayors and councils. Many cities joined together in leagues, such as the Swabian League of southern Germany, to handle matters of both business and defense—including defense against too much control by the Holy Roman Emperor.

FRANCE, SPAIN, AND ENGLAND

Farther west in Europe, royal rule was becoming stronger. In France at the beginning of the Renaissance, nobles who governed large counties barely recognized the French king's authority over them. But in 1461 Louis XI became king and began a program to destroy the nobles' power. By making and breaking laws to suit his own purposes, seizing nobles' landholdings, and conquering those who tried to resist his authority, he brought nearly all of France firmly under his control within two decades. Louis made royal power absolute and unlimited in France.

A similar process occurred in Spain, where there were four distinct kingdoms: Navarre, Aragon, Castile, and Granada. The marriage of Ferdinand of Aragon and Isabella of Castile joined their two realms in 1469. In 1492 the royal pair conquered Granada, putting an end to seven centuries of Muslim rule in southern Spain. In 1512 Ferdinand took over

Holy Roman Emperor Maximilian I, Mary of Burgundy, and their family. Between the emperor and his wife stands their son Philip the Fair, who became king of Spain thanks to his marriage to Juana, the daughter of Queen Isabella and King Ferdinand. In the front center of this royal family portrait is Philip and Juana's son Charles, who would grow up to be king of Spain and the Holy Roman Emperor.

Navarre, making Spain all one kingdom. Ferdinand and Isabella began a line of powerful Spanish monarchs. Their grandson Charles became not only king of Spain but also Holy Roman Emperor, in addition to inheriting the Low Countries (modern Belgium, Luxembourg, and the Netherlands) and Burgundy (now eastern France) from his father, the duke of Burgundy.

Other nations, too, were headed by extraordinary rulers: King Henry VIII and Queen Elizabeth I of England, and King Francis I of France, stand out as some of the major figures of the age. Such monarchs resisted old tendencies to allow local governments almost complete independence. Instead, they held the reins of power firmly in their own royal hands. They promoted the idea of the state and its ruler being one and the same. Encouraging their subjects' loyalty to themselves, they also encouraged the strong development of a sense of nationhood.

The Other Empire

The invention of the printing press, the exploration of a previously unknown continent, the formation of rival Christian churches—these three events made an absolute break between Europe's medieval past and modern future. Europeans of the Renaissance would probably have added a fourth earth-shattering event to this list, and that was the conquest of Constantinople by the Ottoman Turks in 1453.

For more than a thousand years, Constantinople had been one of the greatest cities of the world. It had been the capital of the Byzantine Empire, the Greek-speaking successor to the eastern half of the ancient Roman Empire. It was also the center of Orthodox Christianity, the form of Christianity followed throughout most of eastern Europe. Constantinople was renowned for its size, wealth, and beauty. And its location was of huge strategic importance, for it sat on the Bosporus, a narrow strait that led from the Mediterranean Sea to the Black Sea. On one side lay Asia, and on the other Europe.

With the conquest of Constantinople, the Ottoman Empire was at Europe's doorstep. This was seen as not just a political threat but also a religious one, for the Ottoman Turks were Muslims. Western European rulers, especially the popes and the Holy Roman Emperors, felt the pressure of Ottoman expansion throughout the Renaissance. There were several attempts to unite various European countries in war against the Turks, but these were mostly unsuccessful. By 1530 the Ottoman Empire had expanded as far into Europe as Hungary, where its advance was finally halted by Holy Roman Emperor Charles V.

One of the consequences of Ottoman expansion was that a number of Greek scholars fled to Italy. They brought with them many precious manuscripts of ancient Greek classics—works that most of western Europe had previously known only in Latin translation, if at all. Western European scholars were thrilled to have access to these classics in the original language. Many Italian, Dutch, German, French, and English scholars learned to read ancient Greek. They wrote

and taught about the ancient literature, translated it into their own languages, and fed the Renaissance revival of classical Greek ideas. A great number of the first printed books were Greek classics. Some scholars, notably the Dutch writer Erasmus, used their skills to study the New Testament of the Bible, which originally had been written in Greek. They made translations that were more accurate than the official Latin version of the Bible used by the Church. Such translations became very important to those who wished to reform the Church.

Ottoman expansion affected Europe in other ways, too. European rulers were very conscious of the Ottoman Empire as a threat, but they also felt a great sense of competition with the splendor of the Ottoman court. Monarchs, especially the Holy Roman Emperor, made a point of displaying their wealth in an effort to show that their states were equal in greatness to the Ottoman Empire. But in spite of the threats and rivalry, trade and other peaceful relations continued between Europe and the empire. For example, Turkish carpets were a common luxury in the homes and palaces of wealthy Europeans. And quite a few European artists, architects, and craftsmen spent time in Istanbul (as Constantinople was renamed) working for the Ottoman ruler. Historians are just beginning to thoroughly study the relationship between Renaissance Europe and the Ottoman Empire, and in the future we will probably know even more about the ways these two great civilizations influenced each other.

This portrait of Sultan Mehmed II, the conqueror of Constantinople, combines European and Turkish artistic traditions. It was painted by the great Venetian artist Gentile Bellini, who spent two years at the court of the Ottoman sultan.

RULING PASSIONS

Whether a state was governed by king, queen, duke, prince, or count, Renaissance rulers all had at least two things in common: First, they were very concerned with promoting an image of power and splendor, for if the ruler was respected and admired, so was the state as a whole. This was important in a nation's dealings with other countries and also helped uphold the ruler's authority with his or her own people. Renaissance rulers therefore pursued various means of increasing their prestige and displaying their power and wealth. For example, they surrounded themselves with luxury; supported musicians, poets, and artists; and sponsored voyages of exploration.

The second common concern of Renaissance rulers was to make their authority reach all of their subjects. This was an especial challenge in large kingdoms such as England, France, and Spain. The monarch was the absolute head of state, but could not be everywhere, controlling everything. It was necessary to

King Henry VIII of England radiates royal power and splendor in this portrait by his court painter, Hans Holbein the Younger.

have a growing network of civil servants who could administer and enforce government policies across the realm.

Since the Middle Ages, rulers had had councils of noblemen and churchmen to advise them. The House of Lords of England's Parliament began as such a council, and by the Renaissance it had grown to sixty members. The English monarch was required to summon Parliament and get its approval to pass new laws or raise taxes. In England, as in many other countries, the ruler also had a smaller circle of advisers and assistants called the privy council. Its members, known as ministers or secretaries, were given responsibility for various departments of government, such as the treasury or foreign affairs.

Below the ministers and secretaries was a growing class of civil servants—officials, managers, administrators, and tax collectors charged with putting government policies into action. By about 1550 there were around three thousand such civil servants in France, for example. At the bottom level of government was an even larger number of workers such as bookkeepers, file clerks, and copyists who took care of day-to-day details.

With so many more employees, governments became bigger, and more expensive to run. The employees needed offices to work in, too, adding new building expenses to national budgets. The Renaissance was also a time of complicated international relations, so ambassadors and spies were on government payrolls in greater numbers than ever before. Diplomacy often failed, and there was almost constant warfare throughout the period. The size of armies grew from between 12,000 and 30,000 before 1500 to around 85,000 in 1570. Armies, diplomats, office buildings, civil servants—all had to be paid for out of the ruler's own pocket. Rulers met their financial challenges by borrowing money from the great banks of the time, selling government jobs to the highest bidder—and increasing taxes. It took a truly remarkable ruler such as England's Elizabeth I to keep the devotion of her subjects even when she had to burden them with more and more taxes.

Two

PALACES AND POWER

Renaissance rulers used grand buildings and magnificent courts to help promote their image of wealth and power. In large countries such as England, France, Spain, and Sweden, monarchs had at least one palace in the nation's capital city. They also owned palaces in other parts of their realm, and sometimes moved their court from place to place.

Many rulers preferred not to live in the medieval castles of their ancestors and favored new, less fortresslike, more elegant residences. One of the most lavish palaces of the Renaissance was Chambord, built in France's Loire River valley for King Francis I between 1519 and 1547. It had 440 rooms, 365 fireplaces, 13 staircases, and stables for 1,200 horses. It was surrounded by gardens and parklands, all enclosed by a wall 22 miles in circumference. Chambord's magnificence impressed all who visited it.

There were other ways in which rulers used buildings to show their power. For example, after King Ferdinand and Queen Isabella conquered Granada, they took over the beautiful Alhambra, the palace of

A portion of the royal château, or castle, of Amboise. Built during the fifteenth and sixteenth centuries, it was one of the French king's many majestic residences. Amboise is also famous as the place where Leonardo da Vinci spent his last years; he is buried in the château's chapel.

the kingdom's former rulers. Queen Isabella moved the royal household to the Alhambra to show how completely Spain had triumphed over the Muslims. Eventually her grandson, Holy Roman Emperor Charles V, constructed a new palace right next to the Alhambra—and he made a point of having it tower over the older building.

IN THE ROYAL PRESENCE

Royal palaces in England, France, and many other countries shared common features. Just as the ruler was at the center of government, the royal apartments were at the heart of the palace. The largest, most public of these rooms was the presence chamber, or throne room. This was where the ruler gave audiences to his or her subjects, received ambassadors, heard reports from high-ranking officials, and held public ceremonies. Queen Elizabeth I's presence chamber in her palace of Hampton Court was so splendid that it was known as the Paradise Chamber. The queen's throne there was uphol-stered with brown velvet embroidered with gold thread and ornamented with diamonds. The Paradise Chamber also housed a collection of precious musical instruments, including two small harpsichords, one made of glass and one with strings of silver and gold.

Next there was the privy chamber, a room for smaller, more private meetings. The privy council met with the monarch in this room. Extremely

Queen Elizabeth, attended by some of her councillors and ladies-in-waiting, receives two Dutch ambas-sadors in her privy chamber. Some people think this picture was painted by Low Countries artist Levina Teerlinc, who had been Henry VIII's "royal paintrix" and was a gentlewoman in Elizabeth's household.

sensitive or secret matters were often discussed with the ruler in his or her bedchamber. Its doors were well guarded, and only the most trusted advisers and attendants were allowed in. Queen Elizabeth often took her meals privately in her bedchamber, away from the great crowd of the court. But, like other rulers of the time, she was seldom left completely alone—even when she went to sleep, there were attendants who slept in her room with her.

Just outside the royal apartments there were usually rooms where servants and pages awaited orders from the ruler and the nobles of the court. There was another room where guards stood watch over the entrance to the presence chamber, turning away unwelcome visitors. The guards also made sure that those who were allowed into the presence chamber were not carrying any concealed weapons.

Royal palaces often covered many acres, with space and rooms to provide for all the court's needs. The largest room was usually a great hall, where all the court could eat meals together. The one at Hampton Court held as many as six hundred people at once. The great hall might also be the scene of plays, balls, and other entertainments. Passageways or staircases connected the great hall with the palace kitchens. Hampton Court had six kitchens, while Richmond Palace (built by Elizabeth I's grandfather) had eighteen.

Every palace had at least one chapel where members of the court could attend church services. Long galleries—wide hallways that were sometimes hundreds of feet in length—provided places for people to walk and get exercise when the weather was bad. They could also gossip or discuss political business while they strolled. Other facilities for recreation might include tilt yards where jousts were held, pits for cockfights (ladies did not attend these), and tennis courts. One of Europe's oldest existing tennis courts is at Hampton Court Palace. It was built by the order of King Henry VIII, who was very athletic as a young man and loved to play tennis.

Gardens of Earthly Delights

God Almighty first planted a garden; and indeed it is the purest of human pleasures.

—*Francis Bacon (1561–1626), "On Gardens"*

In Renaissance Europe, gardening became an art form. Gardens provided not only fruits, vegetables, and herbs for the table, but also gave nobles new places to express and enjoy their ideas of beauty. Gardens were carefully designed to provide picturesque views, shady arbors, and avenues of trees for strolling under. There were hedges clipped into artful shapes, colorful plantings of flowers, grassy lawns, terraces and pavilions, fountains and ponds, statues, and marble benches to rest on while enjoying all of this beauty. Some gardens featured "wilderness" areas, made to look like wild forest, and grottos, artificial cavelike structures decorated with crystals and shells. Many nobles began collecting rare and exotic plants in their gardens, and some also housed menageries, small zoos that featured wildlife from far-off lands. Naturally, such gardens were very large—Hampton Court Palace in England, for example, had sixty acres of gardens. These were safe, welcoming places to relax away from the pressures of government and court life.

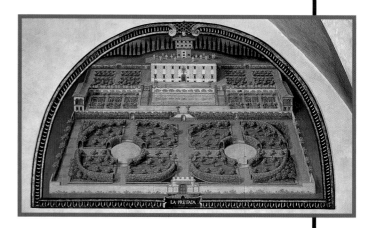

This painting shows how the large formal gardens at one of the Medici family's villas looked in 1599.

DUCAL GRANDEUR

In Italy's city-states, as in the kingdoms to the north and west, rulers displayed their wealth and power in grand palaces. They also had villas in the Italian countryside where they could go to relax, to get away from the cares of government, to escape the city's summer heat, or to enjoy the beauties of nature.

Italian nobles governed from the hearts of their cities, where they sometimes had more than one palace. For example, in the 1520s Federigo Gonzaga II of Mantua had a lavish new palace built for himself on the edge of the city. Called the Palazzo del Te, it was within walking distance of the

A group portrait of the Gonzaga family, rulers of Mantua, with some of their courtiers and servants. This fresco, one of many that decorated the walls of Mantua's ducal palace, was painted around 1470 by the great Andrea Mantegna, who was court artist to the Gonzaga family for more than forty years.

ducal palace where Federigo conducted government business. The new palace was a retreat where he could enjoy himself and entertain friends and guests. One of his first guests at the Palazzo del Te was Emperor Charles V. The emperor was so impressed by Federigo's display of wealth and importance that he raised him from the rank of marquis to duke.

Italian palaces did not follow a set pattern. The dukes of Milan ruled from the city's medieval castle-fortress. In contrast, the duke of Urbino's residence, built during the 1470s, was "more like a city than a mere palace," according to a prominent writer of the time. This large and imposing palace was constructed in the center of Urbino. It was a complex of a number of connected buildings arranged around three spacious courtyards. The duke's pride was his *studiolo,* a sumptuously painted room that was devoted to his huge collection of books.

The Medici palace in Florence, completed in the 1450s, also drew comments on its grandeur—one writer remarked that it was "a palace that throws even the Colosseum at Rome into the shade." Iron gates led from the street into the inner courtyard of the massive stone building. On the ground floor were offices for the family's merchant and banking business, a banquet hall, and a chapel, with a floor of inlaid marble and walls painted with frescoes by one of Florence's leading artists. The next floor had a large reception room where city officials, citizens, ambassadors from other cities, and the like could meet with the head of the Medici family. Other rooms on the palace's upper floors included bedrooms for as many as fifty people, including servants and guests as well as the family. The privileged members of the household could stroll around a loggia, or covered balcony, that looked out over the main courtyard. Visitors were often taken to the *studiolo* to admire the Medicis' collection of books and precious gems. But it was the palace's everyday conveniences that most impressed one visiting writer. After describing all the kitchens, pantries, storerooms, wells, and latrines, he remarked with approval that the builder had "not left out anything that is convenient."

Three

COURTLY COMMUNITIES

A Renaissance court had two important, overlapping roles. First, it was the household of the ruler. The household included all sorts of servants and officials to take care of the ruler's, and his or her family's, needs. There were guards, personal attendants, secretaries, and bookkeepers; cooks, waiters, and entertainers. Horses, dogs, and falcons used for hunting—a favorite sport—had to be cared for. Palaces needed to be cleaned and kept in good repair, and gardens had to be tended. It took a huge number of people to meet all these needs—for example, about eight hundred in the small court of the duke of Mantua, and nearly two thousand in the court of the French king.

In addition to being the greatest household in the state, the court was also the seat of government. Day-to-day administrative tasks might be carried out in buildings designed for that use alone. But actual government decisions were made in the ruler's palace itself, where the ruler consulted with heads of departments and other leading members of the court.

A Noble Household

A Renaissance court was a household made up of government officials, advisers, servants, visiting ambassadors, family members, churchmen, entertainers, and others. At the center of the court, of course, was the ruler. When the ruler traveled—for instance, from a city palace to a villa or hunting lodge in the countryside—much of the court went along.

The household of Duke Galeazzo Maria Sforza of Milan provides a good example of the number and kinds of people who could be found at court. The duke's "inner household" included four "best friends," valets, footmen, pageboys, and other personal servants. The duchess also had an array of attendants, including gentlemen, lady companions, chambermaids, and her old nurse. The ducal children were served by governesses, tutors, wet nurses, and others. Many of the duke's relatives—brothers, sisters, aunts, uncles, and cousins—also lived at court, along with their servants and attendants.

There were a number of specialized servants in the duke's household: an apothecary, a perfume maker, a surgeon, and physicians; tailors, shoemakers, huntsmen, and kennel keepers; tennis players, trumpet players, and jesters. An official called the Master of Works oversaw the artists and engineers employed by the duke. The Master of Stables oversaw the grooms and others who took care of the horses. Seneschals were in charge of the servants responsible for the cleaning and upkeep of the duke's various homes. Stewards supervised the many kitchen workers and dining servants. The duke's household also included priests, along with singers and musicians to provide music for religious services.

Among the government personnel at Duke Galeazzo Maria's court were the members of his privy council and council of justice, diplomats, chancellors, tax officials, judges, administrators, and secretaries. There were a number of gentlemen courtiers who could be assigned various tasks and missions as needed. Ambassadors and dignitaries from other states also lived at or visited the

duke's court. Then there were all the military personnel who served the duke: the Commissioner of Armed Forces, the army commanders, the ducal guards, the messengers, and others.

A royal or noble household had a large staff, which included guards and soldiers such as this young man, who is armed with both a sword and a halberd, a staff with a metal pike on its end.

COUNCILLORS AND FAVOR SEEKERS

The most important members of a royal court were the privy council. Some rulers relied on this council more than others. Even in a single country, the number of councillors and the frequency of their meetings could vary. In England, for example, Queen Mary I had as many as sixty privy councillors. Her sister and successor, Elizabeth I, had only thirteen to fifteen men on her council. At first she met with them three times a week, but by the end of her reign she was meeting with the council every day.

A man could serve as a trusted adviser on such a council without being nobly born. Elizabeth's principal secretary, the councillor she depended on most, was William Cecil, a gentleman lawyer. Eventually Elizabeth raised him to the noble rank of baron and gave him the post of Lord Treasurer of England. The possibility of this kind of advancement drew many gentlemen to royal and noble courts.

William Cecil, Lord Burghley, Queen Elizabeth's most trusted adviser. He shared the queen's love of learning, and the two often discussed classical literature as well as affairs of state.

Rulers had the power to give out all sorts of honors, offices, promotions, commissions, and favors. The greatest noblemen, with extensive lands and lavish residences of their own, often lived at their monarch's court for at least part of the year. Whether or not they received any important appointment or great favor from the ruler, just being at court added a certain distinction and brilliance to their reputations. There were always numerous men of lesser rank—gentlemen, knights, and younger sons of the nobility—at court hoping for recognition, seeking government posts, or looking for ways to advance their careers. The charming Robert Dudley was a courtier of this kind. He was Elizabeth I's Master of the Horse, in charge of the royal stables. He delighted the queen with his wit, his liveliness, and his skills in horsemanship, jousting, dancing, and languages. She singled him out as a favorite and eventually made him earl of Leicester.

Some favor seekers had serious projects in mind. When Christopher Columbus of Genoa, Italy, wanted to find a route to Asia by sailing westward across the Atlantic, he went first to the king of Portugal for support. The Portuguese, however, were already spending their money on explorations around the coast of Africa. Columbus went next to the king and queen of Spain. Ferdinand and Isabella kept Columbus in their service for five years before they finally decided to fund his voyage. Other rulers also welcomed explorers to their courts. For example, Elizabeth I gave a knighthood to Francis Drake after he successfully sailed all the way around the earth.

COURTING CREATIVITY

Many writers came to court hoping to find royal or noble patrons. Even though the printing press made it possible to get books into the hands of more people than ever before, most authors earned little or nothing from the sales of their books. Instead, writers often dedicated their works—in

Singing and playing a musical instrument were recommended accomplishments for ladies. Although most courts generally had a staff of professional singers and musicians, music was a popular pastime for many noble women and men. These three ladies seem to be concentrating hard on learning a new song together. Later, perhaps, they may perform the piece for a group of their friends.

words of glowing praise—to wealthy, distinguished, influential individuals. The recipients of these dedications often returned the compliment by giving writers gifts of money or assistance with their careers.

Some Renaissance rulers sought out writers to be part of their court. Writers could provide poems and plays to entertain the court, histories to glorify the great deeds of the ruler's family and the state, translations and studies of ancient classics, or books of advice and guidance. Baldassare Castiglione lived at the courts of Milan, Mantua, and Urbino, where he wrote *The Courtier*, one of the Renaissance's most famous and popular works of literature. In it he described the ideal accomplishments, qualities, and behavior for men and women at court. Many writers at court also served as teachers for the ruler's children, or they might take on duties such as private secretary or royal ambassador. Thomas More, a gifted scholar as well as the author of *Utopia* (a book that described an imaginary place with a perfect society) and other works, belonged to the court of Henry VIII. Henry gave More a number of government posts, a knighthood, and eventually made him Lord Chancellor of England. On the other hand, the renowned Dutch writer and scholar Erasmus turned down generous invitations to live at the courts of the duke of Bavaria and the kings of England, France, and Spain, preferring to be free to go where he pleased.

Musicians, singers, and composers were also part of court life, providing music for entertainment, processions, celebrations, dancing, and church services. They also might give music lessons to both children and adults at court, because the ideal nobleman or lady was expected to be skilled at singing or playing an instrument. Nearly every court employed musicians, sometimes dozens of them. The courts of the dukes of Burgundy, the dukes of Ferrara, the kings of France, and the Holy Roman Emperors were especially notable as thriving centers of music where the greatest composers lived and worked.

A Genius
and His Patrons

Think of the great figures of the Renaissance, and one of the first people who comes to mind is probably Leonardo da Vinci. Artist, architect, inventor, engineer—Leonardo was all these and more. His genius was well known in his own lifetime, and his talents were sought after by princely patrons.

Leonardo began his career in Florence, where his paintings were admired by Lorenzo de' Medici. In 1482, when Leonardo was thirty years old, Lorenzo sent him as a kind of goodwill ambassador to the court of Ludovico Sforza in Milan. Ludovico was an intelligent, cultured, talented man who enjoyed being surrounded by artists and scholars. He was also ambitious and eager to glorify his family. Leonardo's first job in Milan was to create a huge bronze statue of Ludovico's father astride a rearing horse.

The statue never became a reality because of technical problems, but the designs for it were impressive. Ludovico was happy to have Leonardo working on other projects for him, and the artist exercised his talents for architecture, engineering, and urban planning. Leonardo designed everything from military machinery to a new sewer system to suburban street layouts. Ludovico used some of these ideas, while others remained only plans in Leonardo's notebooks full of sketches and diagrams.

Leonardo was popular at court. He designed new houses for many of Ludovico's courtiers. The artist also played a key role in Milan's courtly entertainments, for which he created stage sets, elaborate costumes, and special effects. Still, Ludovico was often frustrated by his favorite artist, who had difficulty focusing on one thing at a time and often took far too long to complete projects.

For his part, Leonardo did not get paid by the court on a regular basis, so he had to take on jobs for other clients as well. In addition, he had a great variety of interests that he wanted to explore. He studied anatomy so that his portrayals of

the human body in motion would be more realistic. He was fascinated by geometry and drew illustrations for a mathematics book by his friend Luca Pacioli, who also lived at court. His curiosity about the world around him and his inventive imagination were expressed in sketch after sketch in his notebooks.

In 1499 King Louis XII of France conquered Milan. Ludovico Sforza escaped to Germany, and Leonardo was forced to go in search of new patrons. He spent short periods in Mantua, at the court of Isabella d'Este, and in Venice, where he drew up some defense plans for the city. While in Venice he also designed a bridge for the sultan of the Ottoman Empire. Moving on, he revisited Florence, then briefly entered the service of Cesare Borgia, the son of the pope. In 1503 Leonardo returned to Florence, where he was welcomed and honored.

Three years later, Leonardo went back to Milan. The city-state was still under French rule, but it was a good home for artists and scholars all the same. Leonardo trained apprentices; studied perspective, optics, and ballooning (among many other subjects, of course); and became absorbed by various engineering projects. He devised a system of locks that controlled water levels in a canal, enabling boats to navigate the canal for the first time. Leonardo's invention of locks was a great contribution to boating and shipping, and it also had immediate rewards for the inventor: Louis XII gave Leonardo a regular salary.

In 1511 the French were driven out of Milan—and so was Leonardo, since he had served the French. After two years of living quietly in a friend's home, he set out for Rome, where Giovanni de' Medici (Lorenzo's son) had just become Pope Leo X. The new pope gave Leonardo various engineering assignments, such as draining a marsh. In his spare time, Leonardo pursued his other interests, designing machines and costumes, studying ancient Roman culture and mythology, creating geometrical puzzles, and so on.

In 1516 Francis I, recently come to the French throne, persuaded Leonardo to join his court. Francis gave the artist a luxurious home, a generous yearly salary, and the title Painter, Engineer, and Architect of the Realm. Francis required little work from the artist, whose health was failing, but simply took pride in having such a renowned man at his court. Thanks to the French king, Leonardo was able to spend the last few years of his life in comfort, security, and honor.

Leonardo da Vinci's Portrait of a Lady with an Ermine, *painted while he was Ludovico Sforza's court artist in Milan. The young woman so masterfully portrayed was Cecilia Gallerani, Ludovico's favorite among the ladies of his court.*

The Renaissance love of music was international, and many musicians, singers, and composers worked at courts far from the lands of their birth. Artists, too, were much sought after, and many traveled away from home in pursuit of their careers. For example, Sofonisba Anguissola (one of Europe's first famous women painters), from a noble family of Cremona, Italy, spent time in the Spanish court, teaching the queen to paint. King Henry VIII's court painter was Hans Holbein the Younger, a German who worked in Switzerland before coming to England. Venice's greatest artist, Titian, stayed at the Holy Roman Emperor's court in Augsburg, Germany, on several occasions. The renowned Leonardo da Vinci spent time at several different courts. On the other hand, numerous artists were able to find work closer to home, especially in Italy. As a young man, the painter and sculptor Michelangelo, son of a respectable Florence family, lived in the Medici palace (also home to a collection of noted philosophers and writers). The duke of Urbino's court included several artists and architects. Among them was Raphael, who spent his childhood at this court and grew up to become one of the Renaissance's greatest painters.

four

COURTIERS AND PRINCES

Educated people in the Renaissance—including many in the ruling class—tended to be very interested in philosophical explanations of life. One of the ancient writers rediscovered by the Renaissance was the Greek philosopher Plato. During the Middle Ages, only one of his books was known to most Europeans. But during the second half of the fifteenth century, Cosimo de' Medici commissioned the scholar Marsilio Ficino to translate the complete works of Plato from Greek into Latin. At this time Latin was understood by most educated Europeans, and so Plato's writings finally became widely available. Another ancient philosopher who had great influence was Aristotle, whose works had been taught in European universities since the 1200s.

Plato, in his theory of forms, described everything in the world as an imperfect reflection of that thing's true form, which exists in the unseen world of ideas. Renaissance writers in turn sought to describe the ideal forms of everything from beauty to religion. Plato himself had written about the ideal commonwealth, concluding that it should be ruled by a king who was also a philosopher. Aristotle's influential writings on ethics and politics described ideals of behavior. To live a good life, he recommended, people should practice the virtues of steadfastness, moderation, justice, and common sense, as well as generosity, magnificence, ambition, friendliness, truthfulness, wit, and self-esteem balanced by humility. The philosophies of Plato and Aristotle came together in Renaissance writings that described the ideal nobleman or ruler.

Two of the most important books of the Renaissance were *The Courtier* by Baldassare Castiglione and *The Prince* by Niccolò Machiavelli. Each author, in his own way, described what he thought it took to succeed in various aspects of court life. Castiglione's ideal courtier and Machiavelli's ideal ruler were quite different from each other. But by looking at them, we can begin to get a sense of what the life of a Renaissance courtier or king was like.

THE IDEAL NOBLEMAN

The Courtier, published in 1528, became incredibly popular all over Renaissance Europe. By 1600 more than a hundred editions, in several languages, had been produced. Castiglione was influenced not only by Plato and Aristotle but also by the Roman writer Cicero's *On Duties*. Renaissance scholars looked to this book as the major ancient resource for how to conduct oneself in a fitting and dignified manner. *The Courtier* in turn was recognized everywhere in Europe as the definitive modern guidebook for gentlemanly behavior. The book emphasized that everything in life could be made a work of art—a true Renaissance philosophy.

Castiglione believed that a courtier's purpose in life was to influence his ruler to govern wisely, like the ideal philosopher-king described by

Baldassare Castiglione's The Courtier *was one of the most popular and influential books written during the Renaissance. This painting of Castiglione is by Raphael and is widely regarded as one of the great artist's finest portraits.*

Plato. In order to exert this influence, the courtier first had to get the ruler's attention, and then had to make sure that his company continued to please the ruler. Castiglione recommended that courtiers have the virtues and accomplishments that would best meet these goals.

The perfect courtier was a gentleman from a good family. He was handsome, intelligent, witty, and tactful. He was athletic, a skilled soldier and rider—if there was no battle to fight, he could demonstrate these qualities in jousts, hunting, tennis, and swimming. He ought to know at least two languages besides his own. Dancing, music, poetry, and painting were arts that he should cultivate, or at least be able to appreciate. And he should distinguish himself in all this with grace and no apparent effort.

Once a courtier had his ruler's attention and favor, he should remain humble and not get greedy. He should not try to increase his influence by speaking evil of other courtiers, and he should never pressure the ruler for promotions for himself or his friends. Instead, it was best for him to let his actions speak for themselves and to wait patiently for the ruler to reward his services. Castiglione concluded that "to purchase favor at great men's hands, there is no better way than to deserve it."

Did *The Courtier* have any relationship to the lives of real men who lived at Europe's courts? Castiglione himself was a courtier, and his writing portrayed an ideal that was based on what he observed—many courtiers throughout Europe did indeed have at least some of the qualities he described. At Elizabeth I's court in England, for example, there was Sir Walter Raleigh. Handsome, learned, and witty, Raleigh was a successful sea captain, explorer, and soldier. He wrote poetry; dressed in the height of fashion; discussed philosophy, mathematics, and other advanced subjects; and conducted scientific experiments. He was a perfect example of what has come to be known as the Renaissance Man, an achiever in many areas of life. There were numerous others like him. Still, even with the influence of the most accomplished courtiers, very few rulers became ideal philosopher-kings.

Princely Poetry

In his youth, King Henry VIII of England was widely regarded as a model of royal manhood. Handsome, fashionable, athletic, enthusiastic about both warfare and the arts, he also enjoyed writing poems and songs. Here is one of his songs, which celebrates a love that is as enduring as the greenness of holly and ivy leaves, which keep their color even in the winter.

> *Green groweth the holly,*
> *So doth the ivy.*
> *Though winter blasts blow never so high,*
> *Green groweth the holly.*
>
> *As the holly groweth green,*
> *And never changeth hue,*
> *So I am, ever hath been,*
> *Unto my lady true.*
>
> *As the holly groweth green*
> *With ivy all alone*
> *When flowers cannot be seen*
> *And greenwood leaves be gone,*
>
> *Now unto my lady,*
> *Promise to her I make*
> *From all other only*
> *To her I me betake.*
>
> *Adieu, mine own lady,*
> *Adieu, my special,*

Who hath my heart truly,
Be sure, and ever shall.

Green groweth the holly,
So doth the ivy.
Though winter blasts blow never so high,
Green groweth the holly.

This portrait of Henry VIII was painted when the king was about forty-five years old.

RULING IN THE REAL WORLD

Niccolò Machiavelli's *The Prince*, published in 1532, was almost as well known as *The Courtier*, but it did not earn the same admiration. It dealt with the problems of ruling a state in a way that many people found too ruthlessly realistic for comfort. Machiavelli saw that there was a large gap between how a man ought to live and how he actually did live. It was desirable to follow the traditional virtues described by Aristotle and others, but a ruler had to be prepared to be unvirtuous when necessary. For example, even though the ideal prince would always be honest and keep his word, sometimes in real life telling a lie—or at least not admitting to the truth—was far better than risking the security of the state.

A ruler, wrote Machiavelli, ought to be manly, brave, serious, and decisive. He needed to stay in shape, to always be fit for battle. He should appear to be virtuous but should be as cunning as a fox and as mighty as a lion. So long as he had the goodwill of his people, he could indulge in virtues such as justice and mercy. But sometimes—especially when dealing with newly conquered territory—he was better off having a reputation for cruelty. Nevertheless, he should only be feared, not hated.

The prince should avoid flatterers but at the same time should not allow those around him to undermine his authority by voicing their opinions too strongly. Therefore, he needed to choose wise men as his councillors or ministers, and not allow them to give him advice until he asked for it. Then he ought to follow their good advice and reward them generously to keep their loyalty.

Machiavelli recommended that a ruler study history to learn from the successes and failures of great leaders of the past. It was also wise to patronize men of talent and to support business and agriculture in his realm. He should sponsor festivities and entertainments for his people, and give them an example of courtesy and benevolence—so long as none of this undermined his dignity and the people's respect for him.

Machiavelli was a government official in Florence, and he wrote largely from his experiences of the ups and downs of his city. He also used real-life examples of European rulers. For instance, Emperor Maximilian I was a poor ruler because he was secretive, frequently changed his mind, and did not follow the good advice of his councillors. Cesare Borgia, who conquered much of central Italy on behalf of the pope, and Isabella and Ferdinand of Spain were successful rulers because they extended their realms with ruthless single-mindedness and cunning.

THE BUSINESS OF WAR

Machiavelli wrote that a prince should devote great energy to the skills of warfare, which were of the greatest importance to both extend and defend his state. This was advice that many rulers definitely agreed with. Sometimes rulers planned military campaigns from their palaces, or authorized others to head their armies for them. Sometimes a ruler led his troops in person. This could spell disaster, for he might be killed—like King Ludwig II of Bohemia and Hungary, who fell in battle against the Ottoman Turks—or taken prisoner. Francis I of France, fighting Emperor Charles V for territory in northern Italy, was captured and imprisoned for a year. He was also forced to leave his sons in Spain as hostages, and to gain their freedom he had to pay Charles a ransom that equalled more than three and a half tons of gold—a huge drain on France's treasury.

Just as such defeats could humiliate a ruler, victory added considerably to a leader's glory. Charles V had vast resources and could put huge numbers of men and weapons on the field. With his brother Ferdinand (who became king of Bohemia and Hungary after King Ludwig's death), he stopped an Ottoman invasion of Austria and drove the Turks back to eastern Hungary. A few years later he successfully attacked Tunis, in North Africa, the headquarters of Ottoman pirates who had been threatening

This design for one of The Conquest of Tunis *tapestries shows a horse being lowered into a boat during the course of a battle. The artist, Jan Vermeyen, was an eyewitness to the scene, for Charles V had hired him to travel with the army and make drawings recording the military campaign.*

trade in the Mediterranean. Even though the piracy soon resumed, Charles's action had great symbolic importance as a victory of Christians over a Muslim superpower. Charles ordered twelve tapestries—the most expensive and luxurious form of art—made to commemorate the battle. *The Conquest of Tunis* tapestries were afterward displayed on several occasions when Charles wished to emphasize the power of his family and empire.

The noblemen who ruled Italy's city-states also spent much of their time, energy, and money on warfare. Some fought to conquer new territory for their states, while others were forced to fight to defend them—sometimes against the vastly superior forces of France or the Holy Roman Empire. Some

Italian noblemen were professional soldiers who hired themselves out as generals to lead the armies of other states. Federigo da Montefeltro, who became duke of Urbino in 1474, was the most successful noble mercenary of his time. His earnings as a general made him fabulously wealthy. He used his riches to patronize artists, to beautify his palace, and to build a huge and magnificent book collection that was admired all over Italy. In this way he turned his prowess as a warrior into a reputation as a generous patron and a nobleman of cultured taste, refinement, and learning.

LADIES IN A MAN'S WORLD

In many ways, the Renaissance court was a man's world. Women had almost no official role to play in government. Many, however, were able to exercise power unofficially, temporarily, or behind the scenes—usually because circumstances forced them to do so. For example, Isabella d'Este governed the city-state of Mantua during the ten-year illness of her husband, Marquis Francesco Gonzaga II. After Caterina Sforza's husband was killed, she took over his command of the defense of the Italian city of Forli against a besieging army.

Sometimes a ruler came to rely on a female relative to help him govern. Emperor Charles V made his sister, Maria of Hungary, his regent over the Low Countries. King Henry II of France depended heavily on his wife, Catherine de' Medici. When he went to war, he appointed her regent of France and entrusted her with supplying his army. He afterward made a habit of seeking her advice on government matters, especially foreign

At most courts there were fewer women than men, but a queen or high-ranking noblewoman always had ladies to attend her and women servants to wait on her. This fresco of two noble attendants and a servant was painted by Paolo Uccello in 1440.

relations. When Henry died, Catherine governed the nation on behalf of their young sons for many years.

A few Renaissance women did have the lawful right to rule. Mary of Burgundy was duchess in her own right, although her husband Maximilian (later Holy Roman Emperor) governed Burgundy for her. Queen Isabella inherited the throne of Castile in Spain; she ruled jointly with her husband Ferdinand of Aragon and in many ways was the more powerful of the two. Then there were Mary I and Elizabeth I of England, and Mary, Queen of Scots. All three inherited the crown because their royal fathers had no living sons to rule instead. Mary I ruled for only five years, and made herself unpopular with the English people by persecuting Protestants and by marrying King Philip II of Spain. Mary of Scotland became queen when she was a baby, but from the ages of five to nineteen she lived at the French court. For four of those years she was married to the king of France (Catherine de' Medici's oldest son). She only returned to Scotland after his death in 1560. A few years later she remarried and had a son. She was never popular with her people and was always in conflict with the Scottish nobles. In 1567 she was forced to pass the crown on to her child.

Of the Renaissance's women rulers, only Elizabeth I was able to successfully govern her realm on her own. One reason she was able to manage this was that she refused to marry. "I am married to England," she once proclaimed. Elizabeth knew that if she took a husband, she would then be queen in name only. Almost everyone in Renaissance Europe believed that a wife must give way to her husband in all decisions—whether those decisions applied to running a household or to governing a kingdom.

SUPPORTING THE ARTS

Even if noble and royal women rarely had the opportunity to govern, they could still play an important role as patrons of learning and the arts. For

Queen Elizabeth's Speech to Her Army

In 1588 a Spanish fleet, the Armada, set sail to invade England. In this national emergency, Queen Elizabeth I went in person to rally the troops gathering to fight the coming invasion. As Elizabeth says at the beginning of her speech, some of her councillors were afraid that this public appearance would expose her to danger. But the queen believed it was important to set an example of courage for her army.

My loving people,

We have been persuaded by some that are careful of our safety, to take heed how we commit our selves to armed multitudes, for fear of treachery; but I assure you I do not desire to live to distrust my faithful and loving people. . . . I have always so behaved myself that, under God, I have placed my chiefest strength and safeguard in the loyal hearts and good-will of my subjects; and therefore I am come amongst you . . . not for my recreation and disport, but being resolved, in the midst and heat of the battle, to live or die amongst you all; to lay down for my God, and for my kingdom, and my people, my honour and my blood, even in the dust. I know I have the body but of a weak and feeble woman; but I have the heart and stomach of a king, and of a king of England too, and think foul to scorn that . . . Spain, or any prince of Europe, should dare to invade the borders of my realm; to which rather than any dishonour shall grow by me, I myself will take up arms, I myself will be your general, judge, and rewarder of every one of your virtues in the field. . . . In the meantime, my lieutenant general shall be in my stead, than whom never prince commanded a more noble or worthy subject; not doubting but by your obedience to my general, by your concord in the camp, and your valour in the field, we shall shortly have a famous victory over those enemies of my God, of my kingdom, and of my people.

example, Catherine of Aragon, Henry VIII's first wife, supported Erasmus and other scholar-writers. Marguerite of Austria, Duchess of Burgundy, patronized some of the best composers, singers, and musicians of northern Europe. Anne of Brittany, married to a king of France, ordered French translations of books by distinguished Italian authors and invited other educated women to court to discuss philosophy with her.

The most enthusiastic of all Renaissance patrons of the arts was probably Isabella d'Este. At her husband's court in Mantua, she surrounded herself with beautifully crafted luxuries: engraved jewels; vases and cups carved from semiprecious stones; inlaid boxes; gold, silver, and bronze medallions; custom-painted playing cards; and musical instruments. A talented musician and singer herself, she employed composers and numerous musicians to provide the court with music for all occasions. She decorated her *studiolo* with ancient statues and also commissioned paintings from some of the best Italian artists of her own time. Books were another passion of hers, and she had a large library; many of the books were produced specifically for her. She exchanged witty, intelligent letters with artists, musicians, and poets and was famous throughout Italy for her learning and her devotion to collecting both ancient and modern artwork.

Duchess Isabetta Gonzaga often brought together writers and thinkers at her court in Urbino, and Castiglione used such a gathering as the setting for *The Courtier*. In the book, Isabetta and her guests discuss not only the ideal courtier but also the ideal court lady. All agree that she should be beautiful, charming, intelligent, witty, well mannered, sweet, and virtuous. She also ought to be good at music, dancing, conversation, and playing games such as chess. Some of the duchess's guests feel that these accomplishments, along with the ability to manage a household wisely, are all that ladies need. But one guest, Giuliano de' Medici, insists "you will find that worth has constantly prevailed among women as among men; and that there have always been women who have undertaken wars and won glorious victories, governed kingdoms with the greatest prudence and justice,

This lady was probably a member of the court of Queen Isabella of Spain. The artist portrayed her with the quiet modesty that many people thought was one of the most important characteristics of the ideal lady.

and done all that men have done. As for the sciences [meaning various branches of knowledge], do you not remember reading of many women who were learned in philosophy? Others who excelled in poetry? Others who prosecuted, accused and defended before judges with great eloquence? As for manual works [things made with the hands, such as arts and crafts], it would be too long to tell of them."

Queen for a Day

Elizabeth I was a busy monarch. On a typical day she rose early and probably breakfasted in her chamber. After eating she used toothpicks and soft cloths to clean her teeth. She might also sweeten her breath with rosemary or cinnamon and perfume herself with rose water.

When it was time to get dressed, the queen was assisted by her ladies-in-waiting and maids of honor. This process could be lengthy, especially if the queen was preparing for any kind of ceremony. She had hundreds of gowns to choose from and, like other upper-class women of the time, dressed in several layers of clothing. Then there were the long strands of pearls, the rings, and other jewelry to put on. If it was a business-as-usual day, however, the queen preferred to dress more simply, though still elegantly.

For morning exercise, Elizabeth generally danced six or seven galliards. She liked to exercise in private so that she could feel free to dance the men's galliard steps, which were livelier than the women's. She might also give some time in the morning to singing and playing music. Then she got down to the business of government. A great deal of the queen's day was devoted to reading and answering letters, meeting with her advisers, deciding what matters to bring to her council, and other affairs of state.

In the afternoon Elizabeth liked to walk in one of her gardens, or in a gallery of the palace if the weather was unpleasant. Her favorite companions on these walks were scholars with whom she could enjoy learned conversation. After this she often rode out in her coach so that she could be among her people. Sometimes, if there were no pressing matters for her to attend to, she would spend this time hunting with hounds or falcons, accompanied by many courtiers.

The evening was a time for banqueting, dancing, and entertainments. Elizabeth did not care for large, heavy meals but enjoyed poultry, fine white bread, and light beer. She often preferred to dine privately in her chamber. But there was little real privacy for the queen. Some of her ladies-in-waiting and maids of honor

were nearly always with her. These companions and attendants were noblewomen or gentlewomen, some of them related to the queen on her mother's side. They attended to all her personal needs, even emptying her chamber pots. Maids of honor slept in her bedchamber, too. (Ladies-in-waiting, who were married women, generally attended the queen only during the daytime.)

Of course the maids of honor had no privacy, either. Many of them came to court in search of a husband—but they had better be sure they had the queen's permission before they got married! Elizabeth kept a close eye on these young women. Keeping them from getting involved with unsuitable men was just one more item on the busy monarch's daily to-do list.

Queen Elizabeth, with ladies-in-waiting and courtiers, holds court in this scene painted by a twentieth-century artist. Elizabeth has remained one of the world's most admired rulers right up to the present day.

The courtly environment gave many women various opportunities to exercise their intelligence and creativity. Marguerite of Navarre, sister of the king of France, not only patronized scholars and writers but also wrote notable books of her own. Mary Sidney Herbert, Countess of Pembroke, was one of Elizabeth I's ladies-in-waiting, like her mother before her. Many learned men and authors, including her brother, the poet and courtier Sir Philip Sidney, gathered at her magnificent country home. The countess wrote beautiful poetry, edited and published her brother's poems, and translated the Psalms and other works into English. Queen Elizabeth herself was an accomplished poet as well as a devoted supporter of writers and scholars.

HAPPILY EVER AFTER?

During the Renaissance, nearly all women were expected to marry and have children. This was especially true in Europe's ruling families. Marriage was used as a tool to strengthen political ties between states and as a means of increasing a family's wealth and reputation. Once married, a wife's most important task was to give birth to sons who could inherit their father's rank and lands.

Catherine de' Medici's story provides an example of what marriage and motherhood could be like for Renaissance noblewomen. Catherine belonged to Florence's great ruling family, but she became an orphan at the age of three. When she was twelve, her distant cousin Pope Clement VII arranged for her to marry Henry, son of the king of France. Usually it was important for a noble bride to bring a large dowry of money or property to her marriage. Circumstances had left Catherine poor, but the French king agreed to the marriage to win the favor of the pope.

Catherine and Henry married when they were both fourteen. According to custom, the pope and the king of France each visited the young couple's bedroom on the wedding night to make sure that the marriage was starting off properly. But for a long time, Catherine was unable to get pregnant. Her failure to provide a son for the heir to the French throne turned most of the court against her. Some people even believed that she must be an evil, unnatural woman, and leading courtiers recommended that Henry divorce her. Like other women in similar situations, Catherine sought the help of astrologers and magicians as well as doctors and priests, but without success.

After eleven years of marriage, Catherine at last gave birth to a son. She had nine more babies over the next decade. Even so, her husband cared little for her till late in his life. Henry's great love was another woman at court, Diane of Poitiers. The resourceful Catherine, however, managed to make friends with Diane, and she was also friendly with the king and his brilliant sister, Marguerite of Navarre. Eventually Henry, too, came to regard Catherine with affection and respect, and their last years of marriage were happy ones.

Catherine de' Medici was the mother of three kings of France, who all relied heavily on her advice. Catherine also had a strong influence on the arts and other aspects of culture—for example, introducing Italian dancing and cooking to the French court.

CHILDHOOD AT COURT

E ven among royalty and nobility, childbirth was difficult and dangerous. Medical knowledge was advancing, but doctors and midwives still had few techniques to help out if something went wrong during birth. No one knew about germs, so no measures were taken to prevent infections, and there were no antibiotics to treat them. Children born alive and healthy were still vulnerable to the plagues and other diseases that were common during the Renaissance. Many families, even in the nobility, saw nearly half their children die before the age of twenty.

EARLY YEARS

The birth of a healthy child—especially a son—was greeted with great rejoicing, often celebrated with a magnificent feast. In Catholic and most Protestant families, the baby was taken to church within a few days of birth

This painting by Venice's Giovanni Bellini shows a baby wrapped in swaddling bands. Swaddling helped babies stay warm and feel secure, but the bands were usually so tight that the babies could not move their arms or legs.

to be baptized. (Some Protestants, though, did not believe in baptizing infants.) This ceremony welcomed the child into the Christian community.

Renaissance babies spent most of their time tightly swaddled in cloth bands. Otherwise, it was thought, their arms and legs might become malformed. They were rocked in their cradles, bathed, fed, and otherwise cared for mostly by servants. The most important of these servants was the nurse. Her main job was to breastfeed the baby, which she usually did until he or she was two to three years of age.* Even though the nurse was a servant,

*Noblewomen usually did not breastfeed their children, even though doctors, priests, and scholars published many writings that urged them to do so. These authors recognized the emotional and health benefits of mothers nursing their infants. But most Europeans held a long-standing belief that if a nursing mother became pregnant, her milk could poison the baby she was breastfeeding. Noblewomen were expected to bear as many children as possible, so their frequent pregnancies prevented them from being able to nurse their own babies, according to the beliefs of the time.

real closeness and affection often grew between her and the child she took care of. This was especially true if the child was female. As a noble girl grew up, her nurse often continued to be her companion, attendant, and friend, sometimes even accompanying her to her husband's home when she married.

Up to about the age of seven, mothers were generally in charge of their children's upbringing, giving the first lessons in religion, values, manners, and sometimes reading and writing. During this phase of childhood, boys and girls tended to be treated somewhat alike. They even dressed similarly, in long gowns. But at six or seven, a boy was given his first pair of breeches. In England this occasion was called "breeching," and the family gave a party to celebrate. Now boys and girls began to prepare for their adult roles in earnest.

LEARNING TO BE NOBLE

Noble families—in particular, fathers—made plans for their children's futures early. Marriages were sometimes arranged before the future bride and groom were even ten years old. A girl might then be sent to live with and be educated in the family of her husband-to-be; this happened to Mary, Queen of Scots, when she was five years old. In Catholic families, plans were often made for a younger son to become a priest or monk, or for a daughter to become a nun. In this case, around the age of seven the child would probably enter a monastery or convent to be educated for the religious life.

For the most part, royal and noble children were educated at home. Since most girls were not expected to play any role in government or public life, their studies were often limited to a little bit of reading and a lot of spinning, sewing, embroidery, manners, and morals. Their main teachers in these and other household matters were usually their mothers and nurses. These girls might also receive lessons from music and dance teachers.

Some noble girls were lucky enough to receive the same kind of instruction as the boys of their social class. During the Renaissance, this education was more and more often a humanist one. Humanist scholars and teachers recommended a course of study using ancient Greek and Roman texts and based on ancient models of education. The main subjects were those known as the humanities: grammar (or languages), literature, history, philosophy, and rhetoric (the art of persuasive writing and public speaking). Humanists believed that studying the humanities involved students' characters as well as their minds, giving them the best preparation to fully participate in society. But even girls who received a humanist education usually did not learn rhetoric, since this was an art that Renaissance women were rarely allowed to practice.

The School of Princes

In 1423 Gianfrancesco Gonzaga I began an educational revolution. He invited the humanist scholar Vittorino da Feltre to his court in Mantua and asked him to educate the Gonzaga children—daughters as well as sons. Vittorino taught in a new way, emphasizing learning by doing more than memorization and repetition. Like other humanists, he believed that education should develop the whole person—mind, spirit, character, and body—and that it was of utmost importance for students to learn how to think for themselves. Vittorino's lessons in Greek and Latin, mathematics, music, art, religion, history, poetry, and philosophy were so enjoyable that his school was known as Casa Giocosa, "Merry House." It soon became famous all over Italy, and noble children from other cities came to Mantua to study with Vittorino. In fact, so many young nobles were educated at Casa Giocosa that it also came to be called the School of Princes.

In addition to the humanities, it was important for young nobles to learn the social graces, as Castiglione described in *The Courtier*. The young earl of Essex, for example, began his school day at 7:00 A.M. with dancing lessons. Then, after breakfast, he studied French and Latin for an hour each. The next half hour was devoted to writing and drawing. After a period for prayers, recreation, and dinner, he had an hour-long science lesson. This was followed by more Latin, French, and writing. The school day ended at 5:30 with another session of prayers and recreation, then supper.

Elizabeth I followed a similar but even more rigorous program during her girlhood. Tutored by humanist professors from Cambridge University, she mastered ancient Greek and Latin, as well as French and Italian. In addition she learned to sing, dance, play musical instruments, write poetry, ride, and hunt. And her father realized that there was a chance she might one day rule England, so she was one Renaissance girl who did study—and master—the art of persuasive writing and public speaking.

Seven

CELEBRATIONS AND SPECTACLES

Renaissance rulers had many cares and duties, but there was also time for recreation at court. Hunting on horseback with the assistance of hawks or hounds was a favorite activity. Another was court, or royal, tennis, which was played indoors in palaces and country homes. This sport was enjoyed by spectators as well as players. Quieter pastimes included card games (often played for high stakes), chess and other board games, playing or listening to music, and reading.

Dancing was a popular way to exercise as well as an art form and a social activity. It also had a philosophical meaning for many Renaissance people, who felt that the ordered movements of a dance reflected the harmony of nature and the universe. Some dances were slow and dignified, while others were quite energetic. For example, the galliard was so lively that when it was danced at balls, gentlemen were told to remove the swords they almost always wore at their sides. There is a Renaissance painting that shows Robert Dudley dancing a galliard

Two girls from a noble family of Cremona, Italy, play chess as their younger sister and a maid look on. This painting was made by the girls' oldest sister, Sofonisba Anguissola, whose artistic skills were well known and highly praised throughout Europe.

with Elizabeth I: as he takes a hopping or skipping step, he lifts the queen high into the air.

ROYAL ENTERTAINMENTS

On occasions such as birthdays, weddings, and visits from foreign rulers or ambassadors, Renaissance courts often presented theatrical spectacles called masques. These combined music, dancing, poetry, elaborate costumes, and "special effects." The performers were often lords and ladies of the court, but professional performers might be hired, too. The finest poets and composers provided scripts and music, and the best artists designed costumes, stage sets, and effects. For example, when Leonardo da Vinci was in France, he created a mechanical lion for one of King Francis I's masques. At the entertainment's climax, the lion opened and showered the audience with white lilies, the symbol of French royalty.

Many festivities featured fireworks. There were small fireworks displays for private gatherings and large ones for public celebrations. Duke Cosimo de' Medici organized elaborate displays for Florence's Feast of Saint John the Baptist. His fireworks were sometimes arranged in the shape of an ancient temple. Once they were set up to represent a scene from Dante's *Inferno*, the great thirteenth-century poem about a poet's journey through hell.

Mock battles, water shows, and processions were part of many courtly festivities. On a trip to the south of France, Catherine de' Medici held an elaborate riverside party that featured a ballet danced on a river island, a boat made to look like a whale, and a splendid banquet served by shepherdesses. Elizabeth I's coronation was marked by a magnificent procession. The queen, dressed in cloth of gold, was carried on a satin-draped litter and accompanied by an honor guard of gentlemen holding gilded battle-axes. The houses along the processional way were hung with colorful banners and tapestries. Wooden stages had been built at various points on the route. At each of these the queen stopped to watch a pageant of music and poetry presented in her honor.

FESTIVE FEASTS

Any celebration at court was bound to include at least one banquet. Sometimes a banquet would last nearly all day. Fish, fowl, and meat courses alternated with servings of salads and a selection of wines. At the end of the

Royal Foods to Enjoy Today

One result of European exploration in the Americas was the introduction of new foods, such as green beans and tomatoes. A New World dish often featured at Renaissance banquets was turkey. First brought from Mexico to Spain early in the sixteenth century, it quickly caught on as an exotic luxury food at courts all over Europe. At a banquet in Paris in 1549, Catherine de' Medici served sixty-six turkeys. The bird was prepared in many ways—boiled, roasted, accompanied by oysters, as an ingredient in pies, and so on—but cooks especially loved to serve it stuffed with a variety of meats and vegetables. One celebrated French recipe described turkey stuffed with Cornish hen, veal, bacon, mushrooms, and raspberries.

Another luxury that came to Renaissance courts from Mexico was chocolate. The explorer Hernán Cortés brought it to Spain in 1528 and served it to Emperor Charles V. Cortés prepared it in the Aztec way, as a drink that mixed water with unsweetened chocolate, cornstarch, hot peppers, allspice, and vanilla (another new food from the Americas). Before long, Europeans were making the drink with water, unsweetened chocolate, honey or sugar (a luxury from the Middle East), vanilla, cinnamon, and, occasionally, black pepper. Eventually they began to sometimes use milk instead of water. So the next time you have a glass of chocolate milk or a cup of hot chocolate, you might want to sprinkle a little cinnamon into it and imagine yourself at a royal Renaissance feast!

lengthy meal, diners enjoyed desserts and fruit. The goal of most banquets was to put on as splendid a display as possible. Giovanni Pontano, prime minister to the king of Naples, explained it this way: "Local and national dishes will not suffice, unless accompanied by many foodstuffs which appear to have been imported, with great difficulty, from abroad, so that a kind of deliberate variety, sought out with elaborate care, is apparent. . . . The courses themselves should be plentiful and varied; for variety adds much to the sumptuousness and provides great pleasure during the meal; and splendour and abundance are not readily evident without a number of courses."

The arrival of each course was announced by a trumpet fanfare. Musicians played during the meal, too, which both entertained the guests and kept the servants from talking. The best servants were silent and subtle—even though they often wore brightly colored livery, or uniforms—and could respond immediately to a diner's merest nod. Everyone behaved according to an exacting code of formal manners.

The banqueting hall was splendidly decorated with hangings on the walls and rugs on the floor. Plates and platters were of silver, gold, and the finest porcelain. In Italy, diners used two-pronged silver forks to eat their meat, salad, dessert, and fruit. The fork was an elegant refinement that had not yet caught on in the rest of Europe. Spoons, too, were still something of a luxury. Outside Italy, even at the most elaborate feasts, people ate mostly with knives and their fingers, and used bits of bread to mop up sauces and the like. Luckily, each diner was provided with a bowl of water, scented with rose petals or fragrant herbs, to wash hands between courses.

Eight

TROUBLED TIMES

In spite of the splendor and brilliance of Renaissance court life, these were difficult times in which to live. Epidemic diseases such as smallpox, cholera, and the plague affected all levels of society, including the highest. With limited medical knowledge and few effective medicines, even common illnesses and infections could be deadly. Death and misery were also caused by nearly constant warfare. Prejudice, suspicion, superstition, and greed brought their own brand of suffering to many in Europe's courts.

PLOTS IN HIGH PLACES

"Uneasy lies the head that wears a crown," wrote William Shakespeare in his play *Henry IV, Part 2*. Few Renaissance rulers felt completely secure on their thrones. They might be faced with rivals who claimed a better right to rule,

Everyone in Europe—rich and poor, young and old—was vulnerable to a great many diseases. This young man may be a victim of smallpox, leprosy, or the plague.

nobles who wished to overthrow them, territories that declared their independence, allies who betrayed them, and similar challenges. For example, Lorenzo de' Medici was trying to expand the power of Florence at the same time that Pope Sixtus IV was strengthening his power in the Papal States. Both leaders wanted to rule the town of Imola, and this began a feud that quickly heated up. The pope agreed to support a conspiracy against the Medici so that the rival Pazzi family could take control of Florence. On Easter Sunday 1478, Lorenzo and his brother Giuliano were attacked during church. Giuliano was killed, but Lorenzo's escape from the conspirators resulted in a year and a half of warfare with the pope.

Some rulers lived in such terror of plots that they made themselves virtual prisoners in their own palaces. Most, however, continued to make public appearances, enjoy outdoor recreation, travel through their realms, and so on. They simply took precautions. Innkeepers were told to report any treasonous talk they might overhear, spies were sent to foreign courts, and suspected conspirators were closely watched. Naturally rulers also made sure to be well guarded by loyal soldiers and subjects. And the formal manners that decreed who was allowed to be where in a palace not only enhanced the dignity of court life but also gave the ruler an extra measure of security.

Shakespeare on Courts and Kings

William Shakespeare is regarded as England's greatest poet and playwright. He was also an actor, and began his career during the reign of Queen Elizabeth I. For almost twenty years, his acting company was sponsored by Elizabeth's lord chamberlain. The Lord Chamberlain's Men, as the company was known, sometimes entertained Elizabeth and her court. After the queen's death the company was renamed the King's Men, in honor of their new patron, King James I. Shakespeare's plays often featured characters who were kings, queens, and courtiers. Here and on the following pages are some of the things Shakespeare had to say about royalty and life at court.

There's such divinity doth hedge a king.
—*Hamlet*, Act IV, Scene 5

This portrait of Shakespeare, made for a shop sign, is thought to be an authentic likeness of the great poet, capturing his intelligent and penetrating gaze.

The quality of mercy is not strained.
It droppeth as the gentle rain from heaven. . . .
'Tis mightiest in the mightiest. It becomes
The throned monarch better than his crown.
His sceptre shows the force of temporal power,
The attribute to awe and majesty,
Wherein doth sit the dread and fear of kings;
But mercy is above this sceptred sway.
It is enthroned in the hearts of kings;
It is an attribute to God himself,
And earthly power doth then show likest God's
When mercy seasons justice.
—The Merchant of Venice, Act IV, Scene 1

I think the King is but a man, as I am. The violet smells to him as it doth to me. . . .
All his senses have but human conditions. His ceremonies laid by, in his nakedness
he appears but a man, and though his affections are higher mounted than ours, yet
when they stoop, they stoop with the like wing. Therefore, when he sees reasons of
fears, as we do, his fears, out of doubt, be of the same relish as ours are.
—Henry V, Act IV, Scene 1

What infinite heartsease
Must kings neglect, that private men enjoy?
And what have kings that privates have not too,
Save ceremony, save general ceremony?
And what art thou, thou idol ceremony? . . .
Art thou aught else but place, degree, and form,
Creating awe and fear in other men?
Wherein thou art less happy, being feared,
Than they in fearing.
What drink'st thou oft, instead of homage sweet,
But poisoned flattery? . . .
       No, thou proud dream
That play'st so subtly with a king's repose;
I am a king that find thee, and I know
'Tis not the balm, the sceptre and the ball,
The sword, the mace, the crown imperial,
The intertissued robe of gold and pearl,
The farced title running 'fore the king,
The throne he sits on, nor the tide of pomp
That beats upon the high shore of this world—
No, not all these, thrice-gorgeous ceremony,
Not all these, laid in bed majestical,
Can sleep so soundlessly as the wretched slave.
—Henry V, Act IV, Scene 1

Gives not the hawthorn bush sweeter shade
To shepherds, looking on their seely [silly] sheep,
Than doth a rich embroidered canopy
To kings that fear their subjects' treachery?
—Henry VI, Part 3, Act III, Scene 5

The Globe Theatre, where many of Shakespeare's
plays were first performed

For God's sake, let us sit upon the ground,
And tell sad stories of the death of kings—
How some have been deposed, some slain in war,
Some haunted by the ghosts they have deposed,
Some poisoned by their wives, some sleeping killed,
All murdered. For within the hollow crown
That rounds the mortal temples of a king
Keeps Death his court, and there the antic sits,
Scoffing his state and grinning at his pomp,
Allowing him a breath, a little scene,
To monarchize, be feared, and kill with looks,
Infusing him with self and vain conceit,
As if this flesh which walls about our life
Were brass impregnable; and humored thus,
Comes at the last, and with a little pin
Bores through his castle wall; and farewell, king.
—Richard II, Act III, Scene 2

We'll live,
And pray, and sing, and tell old tales, and laugh
At gilded butterflies, and hear poor rogues
Talk of our court news, and we'll talk with them too—
Who loses and who wins, who's in, who's out.
—King Lear, Act V, Scene 3

Vain pomp and glory of this world, I hate ye!
I feel my heart new opened. O, how wretched
Is that poor man that hangs on princes' favours!
—Henry VIII, Act III, Scene 2

Richard Tarlton, one of
Renaissance England's most
popular comic actors, playing a
pipe and tabor

WARRING RELIGIONS

European rulers had always fought wars to conquer new territory, defend themselves, put down threats to their power, and the like. But the Renaissance saw the rise of a new cause of warfare. By the mid-sixteenth century, the Reformation had produced fierce hostilities among the powers of Europe. Some regions, especially Germany, were deeply torn apart as one portion of the population embraced Protestantism while another remained Catholic. It seemed that the two branches of Christianity had differences that could not be bridged, for the Catholic Church insisted on the absolute authority of the pope over all Christians. Protestants had

Some Protestant groups violently objected to the elaborate decoration of Catholic churches. This picture shows one such group smashing a church's stained-glass windows and pulling down its statues.

many differences among themselves, but all agreed in completely rejecting the pope's supremacy.

Protestant states and Catholic states saw each other as enemies. Perhaps even worse, there were often religious conflicts between rulers and their own subjects. The people of a country or city-state were generally expected to follow the religion of their ruler. This could lead to confusion at best, and tragedy at worst. When Ferdinand and Isabella conquered Muslim Granada in 1492, they forced all Muslims and Jews in Spain to either convert to Christianity or leave the country. After the Reformation, Spain did not tolerate Protestants within its borders either. And when Spanish adventurers began to conquer lands in the Americas, they were firmly instructed to take Catholic priests with them to convert the native people to Christianity.

Renaissance England provides another example of the effects religious conflict could have on a nation. When Martin Luther posted his Ninety-five Theses, King Henry VIII wrote such an eloquent response to the protest that the pope named him Defender of the Faith. Later, however, the pope refused to grant Henry's request for a divorce from his first wife. Henry rejected the pope's authority and founded the Church of England, with himself at its head. His son, Edward VI, a sickly boy, upheld this new Protestant church during his short reign. Mary I, Henry's oldest daughter, then ascended the throne. She had remained a Catholic and was determined to reestablish Catholicism in England. The queen's persecutions of Protestants earned her the nickname Bloody Mary. She suspected that her sister, Elizabeth, was involved in a Protestant revolt and had her imprisoned. Elizabeth was released only at Mary's death.

Elizabeth took the throne as a Protestant ruler, restoring the Church of England. Most English people supported her religious choice, for they looked on the pope as a foreign power. But like her father before her, Elizabeth faced revolts by Catholic nobles and executed some of them. There were also plots to put her Catholic cousin, Mary, Queen of Scots, on the English throne. Spain, one of the staunchest Catholic countries, was backing many of the rebels against Elizabeth and was also making plans to invade England. As a result, practicing Catholicism could be regarded as an act of treason. Catholics were spied on and regarded with extreme suspicion. Some—especially men who went to other countries to become priests and then secretly returned to England—were tortured and executed as traitors. But Elizabeth basically tolerated Catholicism, so long as its followers remained loyal to her and practiced their faith quietly.

Another queen of the time, Catherine de' Medici, also struggled with religious issues. Catherine was a faithful Catholic, but she had great sympathy for France's Protestant minority—it filled her with pity and compassion to see them persecuted. Shortly after she became regent of France for her second son, she organized a discussion between Catholic and Protestant leaders. The next year she wrote an edict proclaiming tolerance for Protestantism. But then civil war broke out between France's Catholics and Protestants. Though Catherine made several attempts to bring about peace, the war raged for more than thirty years. Yet for the rest of her life, the queen continued to promote the idea that different religions must be able to coexist—diversity must be tolerated, for the peace, stability, and general good of the nation. It was a noble vision.

The City

One

AT THE HEART OF IT ALL

During most of European history, including the time we call the Renaissance, the majority of people lived in the country and worked at farming and related jobs. But since the Middle Ages, the number and size of cities in Europe had been steadily growing. By 1600, just under 10 percent of western Europeans lived in urban areas—except in the Low Countries, where fully half the people were city dwellers.

Cities were still rather small by today's standards. They generally had populations of several thousand at most. But they were growing all the time, not only in size but also in importance. Cities were centers of religion, trade, government, and the arts. Urban life was at the heart of Renaissance culture in many ways.

ANCIENT INSPIRATIONS

Italy is considered the birthplace of the Renaissance. Yet Italy as we know it did not even exist during this period. Instead of one unified nation, the Italian

The Plaza of the Old Market in Florence, Italy. Public squares like this were important social and business centers for Renaissance city dwellers.

peninsula was occupied by about 250 more or less independent states. Most of these were city-states that governed themselves and the surrounding country-side. Many Italian city-states were quite small, but a few controlled consider-able territory, including other cities as well as country villages. The city of Venice even had colonies on the Balkan Peninsula and in the Greek islands.

How Big Was a Big City?

Our largest cities today have populations in the millions, but Renaissance cities tended to be a good deal smaller. In fact, many communities regarded as cities had only two thousand or three thousand inhabitants. Population levels sometimes changed dramatically, too, due to war, disease, and other factors. It is difficult to get reliable figures for many towns for the same time period, but the estimates below will give some idea of the size of big cities in the Renaissance.

Naples: 300,000 in the late 1500s—Europe's largest city
Paris: 180,000 in the 1590s
Venice: 130,000 people in 1540; 170,000 in 1576 before a terrible outbreak of plague, and afterward 120,000
Antwerp: 100,000–200,000 in its prime, 1477–1576
Rome and **Florence:** 50,000–60,000 people in 1527
Lyons: 50,000 in the mid-1500s
Amsterdam: 30,000 in 1530
Cologne: 20,000 in the late 1400s
Nuremberg: 20,000 in the 1500s
London: 12,000 in 1550; 200,000 in 1600
Geneva: 10,300 in 1537; 13,000 in 1589

Italy's history of urban development stretched all the way back to ancient Greece and Rome. Both of these civilizations had an urban focus, with government and other institutions centered in cities. Greece had colonized southern Italy, including the island of Sicily. Then the city of Rome gained greater and greater power, taking over existing cities in Italy and establishing new ones of its own.

After the Roman Empire fell (in the fifth century), numerous buildings, monuments, and works of art and literature remained. These things constantly reminded Italians of the great urban civilizations of the past. The Renaissance in Italy was largely inspired by the desire to rediscover and re-create the glories of ancient Greece and Rome. Ancient cities and their achievements set the standard for Renaissance writers, rulers, architects, and artists.

THE CITY AS STATE IN ITALY

For about half of its thousand-year history, ancient Rome had been a republic. Two of Italy's greatest city-states, Florence and Venice, were also republics. Proudly claiming to follow the Roman model, over time each of these cities had worked out its own distinctive form of republican government. Venice's legislative body was a Great Council made up of all the adult male members of the city's noble families. The councillors elected the numerous officials who were responsible for the executive and judicial functions of the government. The ruling body of Florence, the Signoria, was drawn from members of the city's major guilds, organizations of artisans and tradespeople.

Venice remained a republic throughout its history as an independent state, but Florence's fate was very different. Even as a republic, during the first part of the Renaissance, it was dominated by the powerful Medici family. The head of the Medici family was the real head of the Florentine state—even when no Medici held any elected office. In 1530 the city-state was claimed by Charles V, king of Spain and Holy Roman Emperor. Charles gave the rulership of Florence to the head of the Medici family, making him a duke. Medici dukes ruled Florence on the emperor's behalf until the 1700s.

Most of the other great Italian city-states, such as Milan, Ferrara, and Urbino, were also ruled by noblemen—dukes or marquises—who owed

Changing Views of the Past

When the architect Filippo Brunelleschi traveled from Florence to Rome in 1402, the city was a sorry shadow of its ancient self. Some ruins served as grazing grounds for cows and goats, while others were used as stables, and still others were hidden by dung heaps. Many ancient buildings had been gradually torn down as their stones were taken away for use in newer construction. Broken statues lay buried all over the old city; when they were dug up, they were often baked in kilns to be converted into fertilizer. Many statues and monuments had been vandalized or completely destroyed because they were believed to be anti-Christian.

Yet Brunelleschi found enough of ancient Rome's glory to admire. Some of the largest monuments, such as the Colosseum, were visible even from a distance. The Appian Way, a perfectly straight paved road entering the city from the south, was still lined with splendid tombs. The arches of various aqueducts, used to bring fresh drinking water into the city, still soared a hundred feet into the air, marvels of engineering. For several years, Brunelleschi, along with the young Florentine sculptor Donatello, explored, studied, and measured the remains of ancient structures. They dug in the ruins, unearthing statues, pots, and coins.

Christian pilgrims had been coming to Rome for centuries to visit the important churches and religious sites there. Brunelleschi and Donatello were at the beginning of a new wave of pilgrims. These visitors were interested in the pre-Christian city—its art, its architecture, its writings. Some made brilliant discoveries, finding works of art or literature that had been lost or unknown since

A view of the city of Rome in 1493. Among the medieval and Renaissance buildings can be seen many structures dating back to the Roman Empire, including the Colosseum (far left).

ancient times. One manuscript was even found being used as a stopper for a wine barrel.

Remains of the ancient civilization were no longer things to be destroyed, recycled, or ignored. Now they were precious relics of a golden age of art and learning. They were rescued, preserved, treasured, studied, and even copied. In honoring the achievements of the ancient past, people of the Renaissance were inspired to make their own lasting contributions to art, architecture, literature, learning, and philosophy.

allegiance to the Holy Roman Emperor but were virtually independent. Naples was a completely independent kingdom that held sway over nearly all of southern Italy until it came under Spanish control in 1505. And then there was Rome. The ancient city was ruled by the pope, the head of the Catholic Church. He owed allegiance to no one, and also ruled much of central Italy, a region known as the Papal States.

NORTHERN AND WESTERN TOWNS

Germany and the Low Countries had many flourishing cities. Like Italian city-states, they usually controlled the surrounding countryside, often including many smaller towns and villages. Cities in the German states of Brandenburg, Saxony, and Bavaria were directly governed by noblemen. In the rest of Germany, some cities, like Cologne and Mainz, were ruled by

Antwerp, one of northern Europe's most important cities during the Renaissance, seen from across the Scheldt River. The bustling water traffic is a reminder that shipping was one of the main sources of Antwerp's prosperity.

their bishop. Others were completely independent, governed by councils of men from wealthy merchant families. The greatest of these independent cities—Lübeck and Hamburg in northern Germany, Nuremberg and Augsburg in the south—were centers of trade, learning, and the arts, with connections to all the rest of Europe.

Some of the most thriving cities of the Renaissance were in the Low Countries, modern-day Netherlands, Luxembourg, and Belgium. Foremost of these was Antwerp, an important center of business and trade. The printer Christophe Plantin moved to Antwerp in 1549 because, he wrote, "No other town in the world could offer me more facilities for carrying on the trade I intended to begin. Antwerp can be easily reached; various nations meet on its market; there too can be found the raw materials indispensible for the practice of one's trade; craftsmen for all trades can easily be found and instructed in a short time."

The strong nations of Spain, France, and England were home to many great cities. Among these notable urban centers were Madrid, Barcelona, and Seville in Spain; Paris, Lyons, Marseilles, and Toulouse in France; and London and York in England. Each city had its own character, depending on its location, its forms of government and religion, and on the kinds of business and industry in which it specialized.

RUNNING THE CITIES

Renaissance cities that were not directly ruled by a bishop or noble family were free cities with the right of self-government. This right was a source of great pride. City government generally involved some form of town council and various other elected officials.

Government could be very complex. For example, Nuremberg was ruled by a Small Council of forty-two men. Thirty-four of them came from the city's oldest, most privileged families, and the other eight were commoners, each representing a particular craft. Of the thirty-four old-family councillors, twenty-six were Mayors—thirteen Junior Mayors and thirteen Senior Mayors. Seven of the Senior Mayors made up a group called the Seven Elders. Three

Hermann Langenbeck, the Mayor of Hamburg, Germany, around 1515. His fur cap and collar show that he belongs to the wealthy merchant class, his book demonstrates that he is educated, and his facial expression indicates that he is serious about his mayoral duties.

of these elders were Captains General of the city, and two of the captains were called Losungers (named for Nuremberg's major tax, the Losung) and were in charge of the city treasury. The Senior Losunger was the highest-ranking member of the council. The laws passed by Nuremberg's Small Council covered every aspect of life—even how many people could be invited to a wedding (no more than twenty-four), how short a man's jacket could be (it had to reach at least to his fingertips when his arms were at his sides), and how to do laundry (don't pound wet garments on a stone—it weakens the cloth).

While Nuremberg had twenty-six Mayors, cities in England and France generally had only one. London was governed by the Lord Mayor, assisted by aldermen and the Common Council. They controlled the markets, courts, and jails; issued licenses; oversaw the city's supplies of grain and water; and of course made the city's laws. They even concerned themselves with the beautiful swans of the Thames River, which flowed through London. The city's officials protected the birds, charging a large fine to anybody who killed one of them.

One thing that nearly all Renaissance cities had in common was that most of the people who lived in them were not full citizens. Citizenship was generally limited to a small number of men. In some cities they were wealthy merchants and leading members of the guilds. In other cities the nobility alone possessed full citizenship. Only citizens had the right to vote and hold office. The rest of a city's people had no say in the government and sometimes did not even enjoy the full protection of the law. One city, though, began to grant citizenship more generously and to look ahead to more universal rights: the first article of Antwerp's constitution was, "In this city all men are free."

Two

THE URBAN LANDSCAPE

One of the unusual things about Renaissance Rome was that it had space for many more people than actually lived there. In ancient times Rome had housed more than a million people, but now there were fewer than 60,000 living in the same area. Most Renaissance cities, though, were packed full. Many were outgrowing their ancient or medieval limits.

Cities handled their growth in a variety of ways. Sometimes more people simply crowded together in existing houses. Some cities began building taller houses, with more rooms to accommodate more people. Venice pioneered the construction of apartment buildings and row houses. In many places, the population overflowed into a growing number of suburbs. Other cities built new city walls to enclose a larger area. For example, the construction of a new wall in 1542 gave Antwerp room for 1,500 more houses.

Florence, Italy, in 1490. Even though the city takes up both banks of the Arno River, houses and churches have had to be built outside the city walls to serve the growing population.

PROTECTING THE CITY

Nearly all Renaissance cities were protected by walls, as they had been since medieval or even ancient times. Only Venice did not feel the need for walls—the Italian city was built on islands, surrounded by the sea, and guarded by a great navy. Antwerp was more typical. Its new wall was high and very thick. There were seven heavily fortified gates in the wall, and ten strong earthen ramparts reinforcing it on the inside. Outside these fortifications there was the additional protection of a deep moat.

Numerous cities had fortresses or castles within the walls. If the city was attacked, people could flee to these strongholds for extra protection. Fortresses also housed troops that could be called on to defend the city. Sometimes this backfired, though, and the city needed to be protected from the troops. This happened in Antwerp in 1576, when Spanish soldiers stationed in the city's fortress became enraged at not being paid. They rioted in the streets of Antwerp and caused property damage and loss of life on such a scale that the city never truly recovered from the "Spanish Fury."

CITIES BY THE WATER

In a community of thousands of people, water supply was critical for public health. And in the era before railroads, trucks, and airplanes, access to waterways could be crucial to keeping trade—a city's lifeblood—thriving. For these reasons, most Renaissance cities were located by rivers. Rivers provided shipping routes and water for washing and other household purposes. The water was not very clean for drinking, though, since rivers also carried away garbage and sewage.

Cities close to the coast of the Atlantic or Mediterranean could achieve great wealth and importance through international trade. If they were on a river that easily led to the ocean, so much the better: they had protection from the sea's dangers as well as a route to inland trade. The greatest

A Renaissance writer praised London Bridge as one of the "miracles of the world." He noted that crossing the bridge was just like walking down the street, except that occasionally he glimpsed the waters of the Thames River on either side.

Renaissance city with access to the Mediterranean (through the Adriatic Sea) was Venice. Major Atlantic ports included Lisbon, Portugal; Seville, Spain; London and Plymouth, England; and Antwerp and Amsterdam in the Low Countries. Many of these ports launched not only trade but also exploration and colonization of the Americas, Africa, and India.

Rivers and canals often flowed right through cities. Venice and Antwerp were particularly noted for their numerous canals and the many bridges that crossed them. London, on the other hand, had only one bridge to link the banks of the Thames River. (People could also cross the river on small ferryboats.) London Bridge, like many other bridges in Renaissance cities, was crowded with houses and shops.

STREET SCENES

Streets, even main ones, were often crooked and narrow by modern standards. They were noisy, too. In the words of one Englishman writing about London, "In every street, carts and coaches make such a thundering as if the world ran upon wheels. . . . Besides, hammers are beating in one place, tubs hooping in another, pots clinking in a third." Added to this were the cries of street vendors and the conversations, loud and quiet, of pedestrians and shopkeepers.

At night the streets could be dark and dangerous. There were often no streetlights, and thieves might lie in wait for passersby. If you wanted to see where you were going, you had to carry a lantern or torch, or you might have

A bustling fish market in a Low Countries city seems to come to life in this sixteenth-century painting. Businesses like this, while offering fresh, wholesome fish, added considerably to the smells, noise, and refuse of a Renaissance city.

a servant or a hired boy carry a light for you. Many cities had curfews, and no one was allowed to be out after a certain hour except in special circumstances.

Many streets were filthy and smelly. Gutters down the middle or alongside streets carried away household garbage and sewage as well as rainwater. In Nuremberg nearly all the streets were paved with stone. In many cities only the major streets were paved. Merchants' pack animals, farm animals being driven to market, travelers' and citizens' saddle horses, and other domestic animals added their waste to the dirt and muck that was already there. Pigs even roamed free in some places, eating the garbage that was thrown into the streets.

Most people during this time period in Europe were unable to bathe more than once a week—if that—so body odors added to the street smells. This may not have bothered Renaissance people so much, since they were used to it. All the same, city smells could be overwhelming, and people used perfumes and other methods to cope with them. People also believed that foul air carried disease, which could be driven off by pleasant smells. For this reason German doctors recommended carrying an apple, stuffed with fragrant spices and herbs, held close to the nose when going out.

HOUSES OF WORSHIP

Sprinkled throughout a city were open squares, where people met to gossip, do business, and celebrate holidays. Most churches had a square or plaza in front of the main entrance. Some of these gathering places were huge: the square before Venice's Church of Saint Mark had space for ten thousand people or more.

Churches were among the most visible and important public places in Renaissance Europe. Many churches were astoundingly beautiful, ornamented with stained glass, sculpture, paintings, and mosaics. There were many styles of architecture, including the Gothic style of the High Middle Ages, with its elaborate stonework and soaring pointed arches.

The Joys of Bathing

Come to the bath house, rich and poor,
The water is hot, you may be sure,
With fragrant soap we wash your skin,
Then put you in the sweating bin;
And when you've had a healthful sweat,
Your hair is cut, your blood is let,
And then, to finish, a good rub
And a pleasant soak in a soothing tub.

—Hans Sachs
Nuremberg, second half of the sixteenth century

For Renaissance people, getting clean could be a challenge. Houses did not have indoor plumbing, or even bathrooms (unless the owners were wealthy indeed). If someone wanted a bath, water had to be fetched from a well or river. Then it had to be heated in a pot over the fire. Finally it was poured into a tub or barrel, and bathtime could start. Because it was such a chore to get the bath ready, usually everyone in the family bathed at the same time (often on Saturday night), one after another. The last person in the tub had to put up with water that was not very clean or warm!

In many cities there were public bathhouses for residents to use. Nuremberg, Germany, had fourteen bathhouses. They all were situated near the Pegnitz River, which supplied the bathwater. Bathing was considered very important—and very enjoyable—in Nuremberg. Government employees got to leave their jobs an hour early once a week so that they

could go bathe. Working people usually received weekly bath money as part of their salary. The city council kept admission prices to the baths low so that everyone could afford to get clean, and children bathed free so long as their parents were with them.

Nuremberg had a group of bathing masters, professional bath attendants who had completed ten years of training and on-the-job experience. They had learned various bathing techniques for health and cleanliness. In addition, they had been trained to cut hair, give shaves, and perform simple medical procedures, especially bloodletting. City inspectors checked up on the baths frequently to make sure that the facilities were clean and that the attendants were working to a high standard.

If you paid extra at a Nuremberg bathhouse, you could get the Renaissance version of a spa treatment. A trumpet fanfare or the ringing of a bell signalled that the water was hot, and you entered the bathing room. After you undressed, an attendant washed your feet, then scrubbed your body and stimulated blood flow by lightly slapping your back with a small bundle of twigs. Next you took a steam bath and had a massage, followed by a round of having your skin swatted with wet cloths. The attendant was also required to scratch your back and probably your head (this not only helped deal with lice and fleas but also just felt good). Then your hair was washed, cut, and combed. After being sprinkled with lavender water, you had your blood let to help cleanse your body of impurities. Your visit to the bath ended with a nap, so that you could leave completely refreshed.

The magnificent cathedral dome (with the cathedral's bell tower in front of it) rises above the roofs of Florence. On a clear day, the dome could be seen and admired from fifteen miles away.

In Rome, one of the most famous churches was the Pantheon, dating back to ancient times, when it had been a temple dedicated to all the Roman gods. The Pantheon was crowned with a magnificent dome, which inspired Renaissance architects designing new churches. In 1418 Filippo Brunelleschi came up with a revolutionary design for an eight-sided dome for the cathedral in Florence. The dome—much larger than the Pantheon's—was completed eighteen years later and was regarded as a marvel. Brunelleschi's achievement earned the art of architecture a respect it had not enjoyed for a thousand years or more. Along with the dome, Renaissance architects took other inspirations from the buildings of ancient Greece and Rome, including columns, rounded arches, extensive use of marble as a building material, and a careful sense of balance and proportion in their designs.

THE MARKETPLACE

A city was not a city without its markets. In many towns, every square in every district had its weekly open-air market, where the people of the neighborhood bought their vegetables, cheeses, and so on. Then there were the great markets set up in the major squares, such as Venice's Saint Mark's Square and the Rialto, the financial center of the city. Peasants, arriving in the city at dawn, brought their fruit and meat in from the countryside to sell in the market stalls. Near the Rialto was another market where fishermen sold their fresh catches.

Many cities had covered marketplaces, some built during the Middle Ages. Paris had a famous market of this kind, Les Halles, two large buildings that sheltered greengrocers, grain merchants, and dealers in small goods. Sometimes a building was dedicated to selling one particular type of commodity. In the Great Marketplace of Antwerp, for example, the Butcher's Hall was where all members of the Butcher's Guild sold their meat.

Such markets filled the daily needs of a city's people. Often there were also gathering places, like the Rialto, for merchants and bankers to do bigger business. Antwerp's New Bourse was built in 1531 as a meeting place for merchants. The rectangular building had a large central courtyard surrounded by thirty-eight stone columns, each carved with different decorations. A visitor from Venice declared that there was no other merchants' hall in the world to equal the New Bourse.

Three

AT HOME IN THE CITY

During the Renaissance, craftspeople and tradespeople typically worked out of their homes. The lower story or front of the house would be a workshop or storefront, while living quarters were at the back of the house or on the upper floors. People in a given business often lived and worked in the same area. All the wool merchants would be found in the same street; on another street would be the homes and workshops of the goldsmiths; and so on.

In some cities, such as Florence, many neighborhoods were practically self-sufficient. Each had its own church, its own square and outdoor market, its own bakery and other shops selling the things that people needed on a daily basis. Rich and poor lived side by side—the palace of a great family of merchant-bankers might be surrounded by the cottages of the poor and the workshops of shoemakers and stonemasons. Workshops involved in various phases of cloth making—Florence's major industry—were located

In the great cloth-making center of Florence, it was a common act of charity to give out clothing to the poor, as shown in this fresco.

in every part of the city, although there were two districts where this activity was concentrated.

Most of Florence's craftspeople who made armor, swords, and shields stayed in an area near the cathedral. Brick makers tended to have their kilns on the outskirts of the city. Here, too, were the tanneries and slaughterhouses, which were banned by law from locating closer to the city center. Cities usually set aside specific areas for manufacturing that produced more than the usual amount of odor, refuse, noise, or other hazard. In Venice, for example, all of the glassmakers were restricted to the island of Murano to reduce the risk, to the rest of the city, of fire from the furnaces used to melt the glass.

HOUSING

Cities varied greatly in the housing they offered residents. In Venice, for example, few people were house owners—most rented their homes. There were rentals for every budget. Rich people could have a luxury apartment or even a whole floor in one of the magnificent palaces that lined the Grand Canal. People with middle-range incomes might live in row houses or apartment houses. The fronts of these buildings were often decorated with paintings by well-known artists—it was important to most building owners to contribute to the beauty and dignity of their city. Many apartments occupied more than one floor, with the kitchen on the ground floor. Venetians preferred apartments that were self-contained, each with its own entrance from the outside. For poor people, the government or charitable groups maintained simple row houses or apartments, some already furnished, with very low or even free rent.

In contrast, most families in Nuremberg owned their own homes. A typical craftsperson's

This palatial house, overlooking the Grand Canal in Venice, was once the home of a wealthy Renaissance merchant. A modern artist has captured the way it looks today.

dwelling housed three or four family members, one or two servant girls, and an apprentice. Even modest houses had plenty of bedrooms: one for the parents, one for the children, and one each for female and male servants or apprentices. The average resident of Antwerp, on the other hand, had to cope with a great deal of crowding in that booming city. As many as ten people might live in a small six-room home, with steep staircases and narrow hallways. Very wealthy people, of course, could afford more spacious and luxurious homes, like that built by the town treasurer in 1554. It featured decorative carvings, brightly colored windows, and a large open courtyard.

In many cities, there was little land available to build on; other cities had high taxes on street frontage. For these reasons houses in places like Amsterdam, Antwerp, Genoa, and Florence tended to be very tall and narrow. Florentine houses might be as much as five stories high, extending far back from the street. There were only a few small windows, but residents could enjoy light and air on a terrace or covered balcony on the roof, or sometimes in a small courtyard. Most Florentine laborers and craftspeople, though, lived in one-room cottages or small two- or three-story houses with one room per floor.

MAKING THE HOUSE A HOME

The homes of prosperous people were sumptuously decorated. There were richly carved and painted fireplace mantels, decorated ceilings, and tapestries and other wall hangings. Walls might be painted with elaborate frescoes, sometimes done in trompe l'oeil ("trick the eye") style, in which the painted objects appeared to be real or three-dimensional. The very wealthiest had collections of paintings and sculptures by the most renowned artists of the time. Collecting was popular among the wealthy: there were collections of gems, cameos, coins, portrait medals, ancient artwork, and more.

Paolo Veronese, a noted Italian Renaissance artist, painted this trompe l'oeil decoration on the wall of a Venetian family's country villa.

Many collected books, sometimes because they truly loved reading and learning, but in other cases just because they wanted a reputation for cultivated good taste.

Venetian glass mirrors could also be found in the homes of the well-off. In Venice itself, maps of the world were popular as wall decorations with people of various standings. All but the poorest Venetians seemed to own at least one or two paintings, usually religious works that were used in private prayer and worship. Many people, both wealthy and middle class, owned musical instruments. Singing and playing music were common hobbies—in the days before recorded music, television, and so on, people often had to create their own entertainment.

Poor people had to make do with very little in the way of furniture or decoration in their homes. For example, a laborer's family living in London's slums might not even own a bed, table, or chairs—just a straw mattress, a board laid across supports at mealtime, and some stools. The family would have a few pots and pans for cooking and other uses, and a few wooden plates to eat off.

But when the well-to-do sat down to eat, their tables were covered with fine linen tablecloths or colorful carpets imported from Turkey. Their food and drink was served (by maids) from silver or pewter plates and pitchers, which were later stored in great wooden cupboards. At the end of the day wealthy city dwellers went to sleep in beautifully carved wooden beds hung with rich curtains and furnished with feather-stuffed mattresses and embroidered silk coverlets. During the Renaissance, a prosperous merchant could live like a prince.

GREEN SPACE

Most cities had a close relationship with the surrounding countryside. After all, this was where much of the food to feed the city's people was grown. London, for example, was surrounded by fields, woods, and country villages.

Easy as Pie

Pie was a favorite food in many Renaissance cities. Pies could be made at home or bought from street vendors, market stalls, or bakers' shops. Filled with meat or with spinach and eggs, a pie made a hearty meal; filled with fruit, it was a delicious dessert. The crust—made from rye flour, whole wheat flour, or fine white flour—was often folded over to make a meal or snack that could be held in the hand, eaten on the go. Here is a recipe for fruit filling for a pie, from *The Good Huswifes Iewell* (*The Good Housewife's Jewel*) by Thomas Dawson, an English cookbook printed in the 1580s:

> *To make all manner of fruit tarts: You must boil your fruit, whether it be apple, cherry, peach, damson [plum], pear, mulberry, or codling [a kind of apple], in fair water, and when they be boiled enough, put them into a bowl and bruise them with a ladle, and when they be cold, strain them, and put in red wine. . . . And so season it with sugar, cinnamon, and ginger.*

The addition of sugar, cinnamon, and ginger—expensive imported spices—made this pie filling a real treat. The wine was also imported, so only a well-off English household would have been able to enjoy a pie made this way. But the fruits were much easier to come by. Renaissance cities had many orchards and gardens, so a variety of fruit could be bought in the local market or even picked at home.

You can give this recipe a try yourself. You will need:

- 2 nine-inch pie crusts (use your favorite recipe, or buy them ready-made)

- 4 cups mixed fresh fruit (any combination of apples, cherries, peaches, pears, plums, or mulberries)
- grape juice
- 1/4–1/2 cup sugar
- 1 tsp. ground cinnamon
- 1 tsp. ground ginger

1. Preheat your oven to 450°F.
2. Line a pie plate with one crust and sprinkle it with a little flour or brush it with a light coating of egg white or melted butter.
3. Place the fruit in a large saucepan and cook over medium heat till it is fairly soft; it should cook down to about three cups of fruit.
4. Put the fruit into a bowl and use a ladle or a potato masher to "bruise," or gently crush, the fruit.
5. Pour in enough grape juice to just cover the fruit.
6. Add the sugar. If your fruit is very sweet, use the smaller amount; use more if your fruit is sour or bitter.
7. Add the cinnamon and ginger, and mix well.
8. Spoon the filling into the prepared pie crust, then cover it with the second crust. Pinch the edges of the two crusts together. With a fork, poke some holes into the top crust.
9. Bake your pie for 10 minutes, then turn the oven heat down to 350°F and let the pie bake for about 30 minutes more. The pie is done when the crust is golden brown.
10. Let your pie cool, then eat and enjoy!

Renaissance gardens were often laid out in artful designs. Here, gardeners are preparing the beds for planting in the early spring.

Some food was grown inside the city walls. Many middle-class people had kitchen gardens to supply salad greens, herbs, and perhaps some fruits and vegetables. Sometimes there was even room to stable a couple of goats or keep a pig.

Wealthy citizens might have large formal gardens where they could sit or stroll for relaxation. Plants here were grown for beauty or fragrance as well as for usefulness. Such gardens were elaborately laid out and ornamented with statues and fountains. But in many cities, such as Venice, there was little room for greenery. Instead, more and more rich city dwellers had country villas set among gardens, orchards, woods, and fields. This was where they went when they wanted to enjoy fresh air and the restfulness of a more natural environment.

four

CITY FOLKS

ousewives, craftspeople, merchants, bankers, doctors, lawyers, students, philosophers, teachers, writers, musicians, actors, monks, nuns, government officials, soldiers, servants, unskilled laborers, beggars—these were the kinds of people who made up the kaleidoscope of Renaissance city life. The city was full of variety and opportunity, attracting peasants from the countryside, businessmen from far-off lands, artists and entertainers, traveling preachers, wandering scholars. All came hoping to make life better in some way—by getting work, making a deal, finding a patron, saving souls, exchanging ideas. It seemed that the city had something for almost everyone.

URBAN MELTING POTS

Over the entrance to Antwerp's New Bourse was carved the motto "For the service of merchants of all nations and languages." This was the philosophy

A tailor uses a pair of large shears to trim a piece of cloth. The various stages of producing clothing employed a great many Renaissance city dwellers.

of many cities, for thriving international trade could be one of the most important ingredients in a city's prosperity. One reason that the people of Nuremberg enjoyed such a high standard of living was their city's location: it was right on the main trade route between Italy and the Low Countries, a natural meeting place for merchants of many nations.

Some cities had large numbers of foreign merchants in residence. For example, historians estimate that during the sixteenth century, one-seventh of Antwerp's population was from other countries. In Venice, the figure was about 10 percent. This city welcomed traders, businessmen, and visitors from other Italian city-states and from England, France, Germany, Russia, the Balkan Peninsula, Turkey, Egypt, Arabia, Africa, and Persia, among other places. In addition, many immigrants and refugees found homes in Venice, especially Greeks fleeing the Ottoman Empire's westward expansion and Jews exiled from Spain.

Some groups of foreign merchants were so substantial that Venice built business centers for them. The first such center was established for German and Austrian merchants, who were required to live and do business there while they were in Venice. This arrangement worked so well that the city also set up centers for merchants from Florence, Milan, Persia, and Turkey. Some other ethnic groups had their own neighborhoods in Venice—for example, the English, Albanian, and Armenian communities. The largest group, though, was Greek, partly because the Venetian republic had several Greek colonies. By the sixteenth century Venice's Greek community had its own church and was partially self-governing.

THE JEWISH COMMUNITY

Everywhere in Europe, Jews were treated as outsiders. People excused their prejudice in numerous ways: many Christians believed that the Jews were responsible for Jesus' death, and most found Jewish customs foreign and incomprehensible. In addition, during the Middle Ages the Church had been very strict about not allowing Christians to be moneylenders. Jews had filled this role, some growing wealthy enough to excite the jealousy and greed of their Christian neighbors.

In all Renaissance cities, Jewish activities were restricted by many laws. Nuremberg, for example, banned Jews from

A sixteenth-century stained-glass window from France shows a group of Jewish men celebrating the springtime holiday of Passover.

The First Ghetto

During the Renaissance, some cities began to restrict Jewish residents to specific areas. Venice was the first to do so, in 1516. It relocated all Jews to a district known as the Ghetto, which had previously been the site of an iron foundry. (*Ghetto* is a Venetian dialect word that literally means "foundry.") The Ghetto was walled in and guarded by soldiers. The residents could leave the Ghetto during the day to do business in other parts of the city, but they were required to remain within the walls at night.

In spite of the restrictions, Venice was still more welcoming to Jews than many other places in Europe. The city's Jewish population grew so much that within a few decades the Ghetto had to be expanded. Even so, to make room for everyone, apartment houses were constructed with as many stories as possible. For this reason the buildings were very tall (the tallest in Venice, in fact) with extremely low ceilings on each floor.

By the late 1500s the Ghetto was home to five synagogues, Jewish houses of worship. The first two synagogues were mainly for Jews from Germany and central Europe. Then communities of Jewish immigrants from the Ottoman Empire, Spain, and other parts of Italy each built their own synagogues. Most of these houses of worship had to be located in the top floors of apartment buildings, because Jewish law required that there be nothing between the synagogue roof and the sky. Only the Ottoman Jews were wealthy enough to have a building dedicated solely to religion. Their ground-level synagogue was richly decorated with wood carvings and red and gold paint.

The multinational character of Venice's Ghetto reflected Europe's Jewish community as a whole. The Jews of Venice and other cities, such as Antwerp and Florence, maintained international connections among merchants and scholars that even extended to the Ottoman Empire. The Ghetto buildings are still standing today, a reminder not only of prejudice but also of a sense of community that could not be limited by walls or even by national boundaries.

the public baths, required them to stay off the streets during the week before Easter, and forbade them to buy any house being sold by a Christian. They were allowed to work only as pawnbrokers, moneylenders, and horse and cattle dealers. The only trades permitted for Venetian Jews were pawn-broking, moneylending, buying and selling cloth, and practicing medicine.

Since a pronouncement by the pope in the early 1200s, all Jews had been required to wear some visible sign that set them apart from Christians. In Renaissance Venice, a Jewish man had to have a yellow circle sewn onto the left shoulder of his clothing; in Nuremberg he had to wear a yellow ring. A Jewish woman in Venice was obliged to wear a yellow scarf, while in Nuremberg the requirement was a blue-edged veil.

Prejudice didn't stop there. During the Renaissance, many cities banished their entire Jewish populations. Sometimes the exiles were allowed to return a few years later, in return for making large payments to the government. Florence, for example, expelled its Jews in 1494, but let them come back in 1513. Some places banished the Jews permanently: in 1492 all Jews were compelled to leave Spain, unless they converted to Christianity, and in 1498 Nuremberg was the first of several German cities to expel its entire Jewish population. Many banished Jews went to Venice, Rome, Prague, and cities in Poland and Russia, where they built thriving communities. A number of Spanish Jews migrated to Lisbon, but in 1497 the king of Portugal ordered all Jews in that country to be baptized as Christians, by force if necessary. Thousands fled—some of them all the way to the New World, where they helped establish the Portuguese colony in Brazil.

STUDENTS AND PROFESSORS

Renaissance cities not only received businesspeople and immigrants—they also welcomed tourists and other visitors. Despite the hardships of journey by ship or by coach, on horseback or on foot, many people traveled for pleasure. They wanted to see famous buildings and works of art, visit important religious sites, taste new foods, meet fellow artists or writers, or simply experience a different culture. A great number traveled to distant cities because they wanted to study at a university.

At the university in Kraków, Poland, for example, 41 percent of the students were foreigners, many from Scotland and Scandinavia. It was much easier to be a foreign student during the Renaissance than it is today, at least in one way: all university classes were taught in Latin, so once you knew that language, you could study anywhere. There were great universities in many Renaissance cities, among them Padua and Bologna (Italy),

Students at the University of Bologna listen to a lecture with varying degrees of interest.

Paris and Montpellier (France), Basel (Switzerland), Cologne (Germany), Louvain (Low Countries), and Oxford (England). Some universities were especially renowned for particular fields of study: for example, Padua and Montpellier for medicine, Bologna for law, and Paris for religion.

Students in Renaissance universities might be as young as fifteen, and they were all male. Usually they lived in the colleges, or university divisions, where they also took their classes, or they rented a room in the city. Sometimes two families in different university towns would arrange to take in each other's son. Foreign students banded together in "nations," self-governing bodies that looked after the welfare and educational interests of their members. This way students had the support of their fellow countrymen even as they received the benefits of studying in a foreign country. These benefits often included lifelong ties with an international community of friends.

Love of learning was a hallmark of the Renaissance. The "new learning," humanism, was founded in the study of language and literature, especially the writings of ancient Greece and Rome. For centuries, education had concentrated on logic and had been based largely on commentaries on the Bible and on a rather small selection of Greek and Roman works. Humanists turned to the original sources, reading them, as much as possible, in their original languages. These new scholars also expected certain benefits from their studies. For example, grammar not only helped them understand ancient texts but also taught them to express themselves well in speech and writing; history provided examples of noble behavior to follow and dishonorable behavior to avoid; and moral philosophy taught responsibility and high standards of conduct. To humanists, learning from the past enriched the present. They believed that while the medieval style of education taught students to think, studying the classics would teach people how to live.

Most universities, however, did not trust the new learning. For this reason, humanists and their patrons began to set up their own schools. In Paris, for example, King Francis I appointed five humanist scholars as Royal

Shakespeare in the City

William Shakespeare was born in Stratford-upon-Avon, England, a small market town, in 1564. His father was a glove maker and wool trader, and also served a term as mayor. After acquiring a basic humanist education in the local grammar school, Shakespeare may have been a schoolteacher for a short time. Sometime in the 1580s he became an actor, moved to London, and began to write plays. His experience of urban life combined with his imagination to help him write the following speeches for three city dwellers.

A Student's Hopes

At the beginning of *The Taming of the Shrew*, a merchant's son tells how he was born in Pisa, grew up in Florence, and now has come to Padua to study at its famous university:

Since for the great desire I had

To see fair Padua, nursery of arts,

I am arrived fore fruitful Lombardy,

The pleasant garden of great Italy,

And by my father's love and leave am armed

With his good will and thy good company,

My trusty servant, well approved in all,

Here let us breathe, and haply institute

A course of learning and ingenious studies.

Pisa, renownèd for grave citizens,

Gave me my being and my father first—

A merchant of great traffic through the world,

Vincentio, come of the Bentivolii.

Vincentio's son, brought up in Florence,

It shall become to serve all hopes conceived

To deck his fortune with his virtuous deeds.

—Act I, Scene 1

The title page of the first published collection of Shakespeare's plays, prepared after his death by two members of his theater company.

Readers and allowed them to teach whatever they saw fit. Lecturing (in Latin) for four to five hours a day, they taught Greek, Hebrew, literature, philosophy, geography, and ancient history to crowds of students.

The influence of such professors was so great that the French author Rabelais was moved to write, "Now all disciplines are restored, languages are reconstructed: Greek, without which it is a lie for anyone to call himself an educated man; Hebrew; Chaldean; Latin; the printings, so elegant and correct in usage, have been invented in our time by divine inspiration. . . . Everywhere are crowds of learned folk, well-informed teachers, and ample libraries; and I am told that neither in Plato's time nor Cicero's . . . were there such facilities for study as are to be found now."

COMMUNITIES OF FAITH

Another important part of the population was the religious community. In Catholic areas, every neighborhood church had its priest and his assistants. There were also monasteries and convents in many cities. Venice, for example, counted 2,568 nuns and 1,631 priests and monks among its people in 1581. In Protestant areas there were priests or ministers and preachers, but no monks or nuns.

People in religious life made important contributions to Renaissance cities. As part of their spiritual calling, they often did a great deal of charitable work. They founded and staffed orphanages, hospitals, schools, women's shelters, and the like. Other city residents also contributed to these charities, both through donations and through hard work. Widows and unmarried women in particular often found meaningful employment working in some of these institutions.

Many city dwellers, especially in Italy, joined confraternities, religious societies for people who were not monks, priests, or nuns. Confraternities supported their members with prayer and encouragement.

They also did many good works, including building low-cost housing, providing inexpensive medical care, and giving dowries to poor girls so that they could get married. In Venice, members of confraternities helped make their city safer by taking responsibility for maintaining the oil lamps that were lit every night on street corners, in covered passageways, and at the foot of bridges. Venice's five greatest confraternities not only assisted the needy but also contributed to their city's fame and beauty by supporting architects, sculptors, and painters.

Five

TAKING CARE OF
BUSINESS

Workers in Renaissance cities included numerous servants and unskilled laborers as well as a smaller number of highly trained craftspeople. Smaller towns might not have many types of craftspeople beyond butchers, bakers, shoemakers, tailors, blacksmiths, and others who supplied the townspeople's everyday needs. But in a large city, there would be people practicing more than a hundred trades. In 1400 Nuremberg's inhabitants, for example, could be found working at 141 different crafts. Among these artisans were goldsmiths, silversmiths, pewtersmiths, locksmiths, swordsmiths, and gunsmiths; brass workers, leather workers, and woodworkers; stonecutters, carpenters, roofers, bricklayers, and street pavers; cloth dyers, furriers, shoe repairers, and clothing menders; and makers of belts, beads, ribbons, wooden shoes, wool cloth, armor, mirrors, paper, wire, bottles, bells, nails, needles, ropes, saddles, dice, dolls, cabinets, clocks, musical instruments, scientific instruments, tools, and eyeglasses.

The production of beautifully painted pottery, known as majolica, was an important industry in several Italian cities. This majolica plate from around 1510 shows a majolica painter at work. He is watched by a young couple, who may have commissioned the plate in honor of their wedding.

GUILDS

In Nuremberg the most important crafts were directly overseen by the city council. They kept a *Book of Handicrafts* that contained regulations about quality standards, working methods, pricing, apprenticeship, and so on. In most other cities, though, these matters were handled by the guilds. A guild was an organization of craftspeople who made all the rules for practicing their craft, including the standards for training, workmanship, wages, and prices. Members held regular meetings and elected their own officials. Often they socialized and worshipped together, and they helped each other out in times of trouble. In addition, a guild might maintain funds to pay for members' funeral expenses, for members' daughters' dowries, and for pensions to support members' widows.

A New Trade

In a large Renaissance city, people followed numerous trades and crafts that had been practiced by their forebears for generations. But in the second half of the fifteenth century, a new technology brought a new trade to town: printing.

Printing was a success partly because of older technologies that were already in place. First there was the availability of good-quality paper. Paper making had come to the West from China, and since the 1300s Europeans had been turning cloth rags into paper in ever larger amounts. Advances in ink making were also necessary for printing to become established, and by the 1400s oil-based ink was widely available. This kind of ink had just the right consistency to transfer well from a printer's block to paper.

The principle of printing was well understood. Woodblock printing had been used in China since the seventh century, and this technique had spread westward. From the 1100s, Italian craftspeople were printing or stamping designs onto cloth with carved wooden blocks. By the 1400s Europeans were using cast metal blocks to print religious images and playing cards, so it was a short step to use such blocks for type. In the Netherlands people were experimenting with using wooden letters to print. But in Mainz, Germany, Johannes Gutenberg and Johann Fust hit on the right technique, using movable metal type. The metal letters could be arranged and rearranged in any order, any number of times. Around 1450 Gutenberg and Fust combined movable metal type with existing technologies, and modern printing was born.

The first printed book, the Gutenberg Bible, appeared in 1455; Gutenberg printed 300 copies of it. By 1500, around 35,000 books—between 15 million and 20 million total copies—had been produced. By 1600 these numbers had increased as much as ten times, and there were busy printing presses in cities throughout Europe.

It could take several people to run a single press, as described by a French master printer of the time:

There have to be four, five, and sometimes six [journeymen] at each press, according whether the letters are big or small, and they can scarcely do anything without one another. Two of them are called printers, for their job is to work the press and to print the paper with that admirable ink which dries as soon as it is applied. The other journeymen necessary to make the press roll are called compositors, because their job consists in composing and collecting the characters into words, the words into lines, the lines into pages, and the pages into complete forms. It is an incredible thing to see that four or five journeymen, thanks to this most excellent art of printing, can do in a day the work of three or four thousand of the best scribes in the world.

A medallion maker. Medallions, which portrayed notable people or commemorated important events, were a popular art form during the Renaissance. Many wealthy people collected them and displayed them in their homes. Medallion makers, highly skilled in casting metal objects, might also turn their talents to casting movable metal type for the new printing presses.

In Florence and some other cities, guilds played a role in politics. Florence had only twenty-one guilds: seven greater guilds—such as those of the bankers, cloth manufacturers, and merchants—and fourteen lesser guilds, which included many craftspeople and shopkeepers. During the time that Florence was a republic, all guild members (and only guild members) were qualified to hold government offices. In practice, though, the government was usually controlled by members of a small number of families who belonged to the greater guilds, especially the merchants' guild.

ARTISTS AT WORK

At the beginning of the Renaissance, artists were thought of as craftspeople. In Venice, for example, painters of pictures belonged to the same guild as sign painters, mask makers, cloth painters and embroiderers, furniture painters, and makers of playing cards. In Florence many architects and sculptors belonged to the guild of stonemasons and carpenters. But more and more, artists felt that they were in a different category from craftspeople. Instead, they saw themselves in the same intellectual and creative world as philosophers, poets, and musicians. All the same, throughout the Renaissance, even the greatest artists produced not only paintings and sculptures but also banners, festival decorations, theatrical costumes, jewelry, candlesticks, and similar items.

Artists had to work for patrons, people or institutions that usually hired them for very specific jobs. It was still rare for artists to create "art for art's sake"—to make paintings or sculptures just because they felt inspired to do so. A church would hire an artist to paint a particular scene from the life of Jesus; a government official would request a fresco showing a great event in the city-state's history; a wealthy merchant would want a portrait of himself.

Even as artists worked to please their patrons, they also explored their own ideas about art. Especially in Florence, artists examined and copied the qualities of ancient Greek and Roman art. Realism was especially important. One of the keys to this was the rediscovery of linear perspective, a way to depict things as three-dimensional on a flat surface. Filippo Brunelleschi, who was a painter and sculptor as well as an architect, worked out the technique after studying the proportions of ancient Roman ruins. Other painters developed the uses of light, shadow, and color to achieve realistic effects.

Some artists began to assert their independence from patrons. For example, the marchioness of Mantua tried to hire Giovanni Bellini to do a painting that would follow her very precise ideas for the picture, from the subject right down to the size of the people in it. The artist's response was that he must be free to paint what he pleased.

Most Renaissance artists were part of workshops run by a master, assisted by his apprentices and by journeyman artists. The newest apprentices did tasks like mixing paint colors, preparing wood panels and canvases for painting, and sweeping the studio floor. Apprentices received lessons in drawing and other artistic skills. As they advanced, they began to work on the master's paintings, perhaps filling in backgrounds and the like. Eventually they would paint some of the people or put finishing touches on nearly completed paintings. For example, when Leonardo da Vinci was a journeyman artist in sculptor-painter Andrea del Verrocchio's workshop, he contributed an angel and some of the landscape to Verrocchio's *Baptism of Christ*.

Some artists were beginning to reject this team approach to art. Leonardo da Vinci usually had a student or two assisting him, but he did not maintain a workshop. Michelangelo went even further, nearly always working alone. In most of his paintings, every single brushstroke was his; in sculpture, his hand was the only one that chipped away the marble to reveal the artwork he knew was hidden within the stone. The painter and art historian Giorgio Vasari believed that artists had a special, almost divine spirit of creativity, which was the source of their art and a thing that set them

Art and Nature

As the Renaissance progressed, people who were interested in art came to take it for granted that art should be true to nature. This is why artists like Leonardo da Vinci so carefully studied anatomy and similar subjects. In some ways, though, art could be superior to nature. This is the idea expressed in the following letter from writer Pietro Aretino to his friend Titian, the great Venetian painter.

I turned my eyes up to the sky; not since the day that God created it was it so embellished by such a rich painting of darks and lights. The buildings in the foreground, although of real stone, seemed made of some unreal substance. Oh, with what beautiful strokes did nature's brush push back the atmosphere, clearing it away from the palaces, just as Titian does in painting landscapes!

With lights and darks she created the effects of distance and modelling, so that I, who know that your brush is filled with the very spirit of nature, cried out three or four times: "Oh, Titian, why are you not here?" For, on my honor, if you had painted what I have described to you, you would certainly have awakened in men the same amazement that I felt when I beheld that scene; and lasting longer, the marvel of such a painting would continue to nourish the soul.

A self-portrait of Sofonisba Anguissola, Europe's first internationally famous woman artist. Her paintings were highly praised for their realism in portraying human emotions.

apart from others. More and more people were starting to agree with him. The changing attitude about the nature of art and the artist was one of the great breaks that the Renaissance made with the past.

WORKING WOMEN

Women worked at nearly all the arts and crafts described above, although their opportunities and rights varied from place to place. Generally women in northern Europe were able to play a wider variety of roles than in southern Europe. Everywhere, however, women had a lower standing than men. Laws, religious beliefs, and even most humanist writings all agreed that men were superior to women. As the Renaissance went on, guilds, city governments, and other authorities began to put more restrictions on women's work. For example, fewer and fewer women were permitted to be doctors—because they were not allowed to attend a university to earn the required medical degree.

Women could not hold citizenship or participate in city governments. They could own property, but it was controlled by their husbands or male guardians. Wives were expected to be totally obedient to their husbands, and could be beaten if they were not. Many upper-class women, especially in Spain and Italy, were rarely allowed to leave their homes.

Among the lower classes, women had greater freedom of movement. Although they were not as well paid as men, their work was valued and could be essential to a family's survival. In Renaissance Europe as a whole, there were women butchers, weavers, dyers, blacksmiths, goldsmiths, moneylenders, innkeepers, glass cutters, bookbinders, gardeners, tailors, healers, musicians, and bakers. Women made shoes, buttons, candles, gloves, lace, purses, caps, pins, barrels, nets, and sails. They sold cloth, books, used clothing, spices, fruit, grain, fish, and more. There were also large numbers of women servants, laundresses, and the like.

In a Low Countries city, women work side by side with men in a cloth-making work-shop. The woman on the left is bringing in a bundle of wool that she has probably carded at home to prepare it for spinning.

In the city of Frankfurt, Germany, alone, women worked in more than two hundred different trades. Sixty-five of these were only done by women. Women-only jobs included not just such things as being midwives or wet nurses, but also many parts of the cloth-making industry, such as embroidering silk. In fact, women played a great role in cloth production. Probably most women spent at least some time every day spinning, knitting, or sewing, either for pay or for clothes for themselves and their families.

Women who worked in the crafts usually did so as part of a family workshop. It was fairly common for a craftsman to be assisted by his wife and daughters as well as by his sons. For example, in Christophe Plantin's printing business in Antwerp, his younger daughters worked as typesetters;

his sons-in-law worked as translators, editors, and proofreaders; and his wife and older daughters ran the family's bookstore. Artists, too, might train and employ their daughters. Marietta Tintoretto worked alongside her brothers in the workshop of their father, the Venetian painter Tintoretto. Ermonia Vivarini belonged to a family of Venetian artists and glassmakers and learned to make beautiful glass luxury objects.

After a daughter married, she might continue working at her family's craft, even if her husband was in another trade. Or the husband might teach his business to the wife; if he died, she could continue the family work. Wives of craftsmen often trained and supervised apprentices, even in cities where they were not legally allowed to. (Since businesses were based in the home, this was only natural.) Some cities, especially in Germany and the Low Countries, but also in England and France, allowed women to become guild members, not only as widows of master craftsmen, but as masters in their own right. For a widow or unmarried woman, having a trade could be crucial to survival.

Six

GROWING UP

During the Renaissance, babies were nearly always born at home. A well-to-do mother would be surrounded by women friends, relatives, servants, and midwives during her labor. A poor mother might not be able to afford a midwife and would have to rely on the assistance of female friends and relatives. Even with the best help, childbearing was extremely dangerous. No one knew yet about germs and ways to prevent infection, and there were few medical techniques for dealing with problems during the birth process. Many mothers and babies died during or soon after childbirth.

If mother and child survived the birth, there was often a great celebration. In France and Italy, women who had just given birth were honored and pampered. In a wealthy family the mother's room was decorated with expensive ornaments, and the women friends and relatives who visited and helped her wore their best jewels. Male friends and relatives, especially in

Florence, had artists make specially decorated plates to honor new mothers. Families in the higher classes especially welcomed the birth of a healthy boy, who would carry on the family name and business.

EARLY YEARS

Childhood could be full of insecurity. Disease was widespread during the Renaissance, and young children were extremely vulnerable. Plague, smallpox, tuberculosis, flu, diarrhea, and various infections took many children's lives. Poor children were also threatened by malnutrition and starvation. More than half of all Europeans did not live through childhood. But in spite of the uncertainties, most parents seem to have treasured their children and to have done their best to raise them with love and care.

Babies were cuddled, rocked in their cradles, sung lullabies to, and fed whenever they were hungry. They were kept warm and cozy by being wrapped in swaddling bands. Proper swaddling was also believed to help the arms and legs form correctly. Most mothers nursed their own babies until they were one to two years old. In the upper classes, however, it was fairly common to hire a wet nurse to breastfeed the baby and tend to its other basic needs. Usually the nurse lived with the family, but sometimes babies were sent to be nursed by a neighbor or by a peasant in the nearby countryside.

Popular advice books encouraged parents not to talk baby talk to their toddlers. Instead parents should converse with them in a clear and correct way to help them learn to speak properly. Once the child learned to talk well, it was time for the mother to begin teaching basic prayers. Meanwhile, the father should make sure that the child was only told fairy tales that would teach good moral lessons.

The best way for children to learn good behavior, according to most advice books, was from their parents' example. Parents should also encourage their children and strengthen their knowledge and willpower so that

Children in Antwerp play with homemade toys, blow bubbles, and pet a tame bird in this detail of a painting by Pieter Brueghel the Elder.

they would always choose right behavior. It was important not to spoil children, but severe punishment was frowned on. As one writer put it, "Force and scare tactics result in habitual anger and fear. . . . The health of the child's body and mind consists in the moderation of his ways."

It was also very important for children to run around and play. Just like children today, they liked to pretend they were grown-ups, blow bubbles,

A Renaissance Game

Renaissance people of all ages loved to play games—chess, checkers, card games, dice games, and others. Here is a game that would have been enjoyed in many Renaissance cities, adapted so that you can play it today.

Shove-Groat

This game, also known as shovelboard, was often played with English coins called groats. A wealthy family might own a special table just for playing shove-groat, but almost any table will do.

Make sure your table is clean and clear; it will be hard to play shove-groat on a sticky table or one covered with a tablecloth. Mark off horizontal sections on the table by putting salt and pepper shakers or other objects spaced along the table's long edges, for example at six inches, twelve inches, eighteen inches, and so on.

The players sit or stand at one end of the table. The section nearest the players is worth five points, the next section ten points, and on up. Each player has a metal disk—a penny, nickel, or quarter should work fine. Take turns pushing your coins down the table. Your goal is to get your coin as close to the table's edge—the highest-scoring section—as possible. If your coin goes over the edge, you get zero points. Otherwise you get the number of points assigned to the section where your coin stops. The winner can be the person with the most points after ten tries or the first person to score a hundred points, or you can choose some other way to decide the winner—Renaissance games were very flexible.

play with pet cats and dogs, and tell jokes and riddles. Hobbyhorses, tops, balls, dolls, and wooden swords were some of the common toys. Popular games included Renaissance versions of tag, hide-and-seek, blindman's buff, leapfrog, and checkers.

SCHOOLING

Children received their earliest education at home. Some parents taught the alphabet by cutting fruit or pastry into the shapes of letters. Children were rewarded for correctly naming a letter by being allowed to eat it. Parents were advised to keep early education fun and not to push their young children too hard, because this might take the joy out of learning.

Between the ages of five and seven, education began to get serious. Upper-class families often hired tutors to teach both sons and daughters. Many upper- and middle-class children started going to school. Most schools were for boys only, but there were some for both boys and girls. In these schools teachers were sometimes women, and quite a few cities had girls-only schools where the teachers were always women. Schooling for girls was more common in northern Europe than in the south, but it was still fairly rare. Most girls were taught at home by their mothers, who instructed them in running a household, religion, and reading.

The best schools and tutors followed humanist ideas about education and made sure to give children breaks from their studies to go outside for fresh air and exercise. The most important subjects were reading, writing, Latin, rhetoric (the art of persuasive speaking and writing), literature, philosophy, and history. Many humanists also taught religion, Greek, math, and music. Girls, however, usually did not learn rhetoric, Latin, Greek, or much math. But whether they were educated in a school or at home, they always learned household skills such as spinning, sewing, knitting, and embroidery.

LEARNING A TRADE

In most areas, poor children seldom learned to read. Their childhoods were brief, because they usually had to go to work at an early age. Some helped

One of the first things an artist's apprentice learned to do was to grind pigments for making paint.

with their parents' work, while others became servants. If they were lucky enough to train for a skilled craft or trade, they usually began an apprenticeship between the ages of twelve and fifteen. Children of craftspeople and merchants often went to school up till this point, then began learning the family business.

Boys did not always follow the family trade, however. Take the examples of the following artists: Leonardo da Vinci's father was a notary, Michelangelo's was a government administrator, and Albrecht Dürer's was a goldsmith. Fathers were sometimes upset when sons did not want to follow in their footsteps. But often, when a boy showed a definite talent or desire for a different profession, the family went out of its way to arrange for him to learn his chosen career. Girls did not have as many opportunities. Usually if they were going to work at a craft or trade, their only opportunity to learn it was in the family home.

Apprentices often lived with their masters, paying for room and board. In exchange for their training, they worked for their masters free of charge. Apprenticeship could last from just a couple years to seven or more years, depending on how hard it was to learn a particular craft. For example, bakers had very short apprenticeships, but printers, goldsmiths, and glassblowers had longer ones. After this period of training, the young craftsperson worked as a journeyman, assisting in a master's workshop, for another three to six years. Then it was finally possible to apply to be a master. Usually the journeyman had to produce a masterpiece that demonstrated thorough command of the craft. In addition a payment had to be made to the guild—or, in Nuremberg, to the city treasury. Nuremberg's city council put one other condition on journeymen who wanted to become masters: they must get married and establish their own household.

Humanism for Girls

Sir Thomas More, probably England's greatest humanist, had three daughters and one son. He gave all four children the highest-quality education possible, personally training them in Latin, Greek, literature, rhetoric, history, philosophy, and mathematics. Justifying the equal education he gave his daughters, More wrote in a letter that girls and boys "both have the name of human being. . . ; both, I say, are equally suited for the knowledge of learning by which reason is cultivated, and, like plowed land, germinates a crop when the seeds of good precepts have been sown." Unfortunately, it would be a long time before More's philosophy of equal education for boys and girls was accepted by most people. During the whole Renaissance period, there were probably no more than sixty women humanists in all of England.

LEAVING CHILDHOOD BEHIND

In the wealthiest families, especially in southern Europe, girls often married in their teens. Their husbands might be in their thirties or older. Usually, though, people were in their twenties when they married. This gave the man time to establish himself in his trade. It gave the woman and her family time to save up her dowry, the money and belongings she had to bring to her marriage. Many girls worked as servants for years to earn their dowry.

It was normal for marriages to be arranged by the families. Advice-book writers recommended that parents put themselves in their children's place and choose for them husbands and wives who would truly make them happy. But parents sometimes selected a bride or groom whose family was wealthy or important, and for no other reason. Occasionally parents even forced children into marrying against their will, even though the law required that the bride and groom both consent to the marriage.

Sometimes a couple married simply because they were in love. Most people believed that this was not a good basis for marriage—it did not take practical matters into account, and love could fade over the years. It was even worse if the couple did not have their parents' consent. Marriage would work out best when both partners had similar personalities, came from the same level of wealth and society, and had the support of their families. Nearly everyone agreed that the ideal marriage was one where the couple liked and respected each other, so that they could be true friends and companions for as long as they both lived.

During Carnival the general order of society was turned upside down.

In some places where the Protestant Reformation took hold, much of this changed. Many holidays were banned because they honored Catholic saints. Some Protestant groups even refused to celebrate Christmas—they felt that most Christmas customs were un-Christian and that in any case, no day was holier than another. Very strict Protestants also frowned on amusements such as dancing, playing cards, singing non-religious songs, and reading fiction. In Geneva, Switzerland, for example, people were not even allowed to dance at weddings.

FAIRS

Many Renaissance cities held huge trade fairs, sometimes three or four a year. One of the most famous fairs was held in Venice for two weeks in early summer. As many as 100,000 people attended it. The city's craft guilds filled Saint Mark's Square with booths and handcarts stocked with Venetian luxury items, among them glassware, mirrors, silk, lace, soap, perfume, jewelry, and furniture. Also for sale were imported goods from all around the Mediterranean, and paintings by foreign artists as well as by Venetians.

Fairs attracted people from all walks of life. Merchants came from other city-states and countries to buy goods to resell at home. Others came to sell or trade imported goods or the products of their homeland. Peasants came from the surrounding countryside to sell a little of their extra produce and to see the sights. Traveling entertainers of all kinds amused the crowds. Even nobles attended the fairs, eager to see the great display of goods for sale. They created their own kind of display, too, processing through the town with their attendants, often by torchlight or in costume.

Although fairs were all about bringing business into a city, there was also a holiday feeling to them. Antwerp's two great fairs, six weeks each in May and August, contributed immensely to the city's wealth. From beginning to end, they also contributed to the city's liveliness. On the first day of the fair, city officials gathered at the town hall. The youngest of them, dressed in red velvet, selected a pretty girl to be the Maid of Antwerp. Seated on a throne, she handed out red and white roses to the officials; the youngest official presented her with a plate of sugarplums, and received a kiss. With this, the fair was declared open. The city was full of people visiting the booths that crowded the Great Marketplace, smaller market squares, and even churchyards. Every night during the fair, musicians gave concerts in front of the town hall.

Dürer Describes a Parade

German artist Albrecht Dürer traveled to many Renaissance cities and recorded his impressions of them in letters to his friends. Here he describes one of the spectacular religious processions typical of many urban holy day celebrations:

On the Sunday after our dear Lady's Assumption I saw the great procession from the Church of Our Lady at Antwerp, when the whole town of every craft and rank was assembled, each dressed in his best according to his rank. And all ranks and guilds had their signs, by which they might be known. In the intervals great costly pole-candles were borne, and their long old Frankish trumpets of silver. There were also in the German fashion many pipers and drummers. All the instruments were loudly and noisily blown and beaten.

I saw the procession pass along the street, the people being arranged in rows. . . . There were goldsmiths, the painters, the masons, the broiderers, the sculptors, the join-ers, the carpenters, the sailors, the fishermen, the butchers, the leatherers, the cloth-makers, the bakers, the tailors, the shoemakers—indeed workmen of all kinds, and many craftsmen and dealers who work for their livelihood. Likewise the shopkeepers and mer-chants and their assistants of all kinds were there. After these came the shooters with guns, bows, and crossbows, and the horsemen and foot soldiers also. Then followed a great crowd of the lords magistrates. Then came a fine troop all in red, nobly and splen-didly clad. Before them, however, went all the religious orders and the members of some foundations very devoutly, all in their different robes. A very large company of widows also took part in this procession. They support themselves with their own hands and observe a special rule. They were all dressed from head to foot in white linen garments, made expressly for the occasion, very sorrowful to see. Among them I saw some very stately persons. Last of all came the chapter of Our Lady's Church, with all their clergy, scholars, and treasures. Twenty persons bore the image of the Virgin Mary with the Lord Jesus, adorned in the costliest manner, to the honour of the Lord God.

In this procession very many delightful things were shown, most splendidly got up. Wagons were drawn along with masques upon ships and other structures. Among them was the company of the prophets in their order and scenes from the New Testament, such as the Annunciation, the Three Holy Kings riding on great camels and on other rare beasts, very well arranged; also how Our Lady fled to Egypt—very devout—and many other things. . . . At the end came a great dragon, which St. Margaret and her maidens led by a girdle; she was especially beautiful. Behind her came St. George with his squires, a very goodly knight in armour. In this host also rode boys and maidens most finely and splendidly dressed in the costumes of many lands, representing various saints. From beginning to end the procession lasted more than two hours before it was gone past our house.

Four camels lead off a procession featuring elaborate horse-drawn floats. Parades such as this were often held to celebrate a ruler's entrance into a city. Religious processions could be just as splendid.

PLAYS

Among the entertainers that came to fairs were traveling groups of actors. A popular type of theater in northern Italian cities during the 1500s was commedia dell'arte. Performing in the public squares, the actors wore masks and made up their lines as they went along. Commedia dell'arte used a cast of stereotyped characters, such as an old miser, a sassy maid, and young lovers. The plays featured a great deal of clowning around and could be very rowdy—and so could the audience!

In Nuremberg, as in many other cities, playacting was part of Carnival, when groups of craftsmen would put on comic skits in taverns.

Actors give a performance on a temporary stage set up at a fair, probably in Antwerp. Behind the curtain, a man follows along in the script, ready to prompt any actors who forget their lines.

These little plays were often improvised and involved audience participation. They became very popular, and the city council started allowing them to be put on in places besides taverns. Eventually there were a dozen acting troupes in Nuremberg, performing plays from New Year's to Easter.

In London there were professional theater companies that presented plays almost every afternoon year-round. When they went on tour through the rest of England, they performed in guildhalls, the yards of inns, or any other available open space. But at home in the city, beginning in 1576, there were permanent theaters, built just for the presentation of plays. The most celebrated of the playhouses was the Globe, the home of the theater company known as the Lord Chamberlain's Men (later the King's Men). One of the company's founders was William Shakespeare. He was also an actor and, more importantly, the company's main playwright. In his own time Shakespeare was praised as England's "most excellent" writer of comedies and tragedies. Today he is widely regarded as the greatest poet and playwright ever to write in the English language.

Eight

THE STRUGGLE FOR SURVIVAL

We think of the Renaissance as a time of great art and learning, full of new opportunities for wealth and cultural advancement. This is true, but the sad fact is that these new possibilities were open to only a small percentage of people—mostly upper-class and upper-middle-class men. It was a long time before the average person felt the effects of the Renaissance. Meanwhile, the gap between rich and poor was growing ever wider.

Various hardships in the countryside spurred thousands of peasants to move to cities in the hope of finding work, but there were not enough jobs for everyone. The number of beggars on city streets grew tremendously during the Renaissance. Many places outlawed begging—offenders could be whipped through the streets, put in the stocks, banished, or even sent to prison. In other cities begging was permitted only under certain conditions. For example, Nuremberg allowed people with disabilities to beg, but they were expected to also do needlework, woodworking, or the like if they were physically able.

DISASTER ZONES

Growing poverty led to increasing crime and violence in many cities. The desperately poor often felt that they could only survive by robbing the better-off. Sometimes the poor rioted, especially when bad harvests in the countryside led to bread shortages in the city. There were also uprisings by overworked and underfed apprentices from time to time.

Religious differences were another cause of urban violence. Protestant townspeople sometimes threw rocks at monks. Objecting to the elaborate decoration of churches, Reformers in the Low Countries and elsewhere destroyed religious statues and smashed stained-glass windows. The great humanist Erasmus described the scene in Basel, Switzerland, in 1529: "Not a statue had been left in the churches . . . or in the monasteries. Everything frescoed is lost under coats of whitewash. Whatever would burn has been thrown into the pyre, everything else hacked into small pieces. Neither value nor artistry prevailed to save anything." An infamous case of religious violence, known as the Saint Bartholomew's Day Massacre, occurred in Paris in 1572, when Catholic mobs killed thousands of French Protestants.

Renaissance cities were threatened from without, too. Many were attacked by foreign powers more than once during the period. Sometimes a city was besieged, cut off from supplies until it gave in or the attackers gave up. But many times armies broke through the city walls, killing citizens and destroying property. Rome itself, the headquarters of the Catholic Church, was assaulted in 1527 by combined Spanish and German forces. The city was sacked, thousands of citizens killed or injured, buildings burned, and an untold number of books and works of art destroyed. When the invaders finally left after nine months, it took years to rebuild Rome.

Warfare always brought other evils with it, especially famine and disease. In peacetime, too, disease was a constant threat. Worst of all was the plague, an unstoppable epidemic. It killed almost everyone who came down with it, usually within a few days. Plague swept through cities more than once

The body of a Protestant killed during the Saint Bartholomew's Day Massacre is carried away by his friends.

during the Renaissance. In London, for example, at least 10,000 people died of plague in 1593 and at least 25,000 in 1603. Plague and other diseases struck in the countryside, too, but they spread even more in cities because people were so crowded together. The poor suffered worst of all.

Urban crowding made fire a great danger, too. In many cities most houses were built of wood with thatched roofs. This was the case in Antwerp, where large areas burned down in 1441 and 1443. Antwerp suffered so many fires in 1503 that lawmakers ordered homeowners to replace roof thatch with tiles and to keep tubs of water by all doorways. Eventually the city outlawed using wood to build or repair any house. But it was not just humble homes that went up in flames. For instance, a fire in 1514 nearly destroyed the whole Rialto, Venice's center of banking and business.

One City's Woes

For about a hundred years, Antwerp (in modern-day Belgium) was one of Europe's leading cities—some said *the* leading city in business and trade. But like any other city of its time, it had its share of troubles. Here is a chronology of Antwerp's hard times:

1441   Fire: many parts of Antwerp are consumed.

1443   Fire: an entire district of the city is completely destroyed.

1477   Rebellion: some Antwerpians revolt against the authority of Duchess Mary of Burgundy.

1480   Plague and heavy flooding

1483   Military action: Maximilian of Habsburg, Mary of Burgundy's husband (and future Holy Roman Emperor), puts down the Antwerpian rebellion against his wife.

1485   Plague

1503   A series of fires

1517   Plague

1524   Bread shortage

1529   Plague

1530   Heavy flooding

1532   Heavy flooding

1542   War: a mercenary force (fighting for William of Cleves) attacks Antwerp, ravaging the surrounding countryside and breaching the city walls before being defeated.

1545   Food shortage

1546   Food shortage

1551   Plague

1552   Two serious floods

1556   Food shortage

1565   Food shortage

1566   Rioting: Protestant vandals loot churches and other Catholic religious institutions.

1576   The Spanish Fury: unpaid Spanish soldiers rush out of Antwerp's fortress and rampage through the city, burning more than 1,000 homes and killing more than 8,000 Antwerpians.

1583   The French Fury: French soldiers, who are supposed to be protecting Antwerpians from the Spanish, run riot in the city.

1584–1585
       Siege: Spanish forces blockade and besiege Antwerp.

1585   Defeat: on August 17, Antwerp surrenders to Spain, losing its historic freedom and economic supremacy.

URBAN IMPROVEMENTS

Antwerp's fire safety laws are a good example of the steps that Renaissance cities began to take to solve their problems. Other cities created fire brigades, or required residents of each district to be responsible for fighting neighborhood fires. Additional public safety measures included employing night watchmen to patrol the streets after dark in many areas. In London they were called bellmen, because they carried a bell that they could ring to summon help in an emergency.

Strides were made to try to control the spread of disease, too. Take the case of plague: people did not know that it was caused by bacteria carried by fleas that lived on black rats. It was clear, however, that the disease could spread from an infected person, so cities passed regulations that isolated anyone who might possibly have the plague. Travelers coming from infected areas were not allowed into towns, or they had to spend forty days in a special hospital to make sure they were symptom-free before entering the town. Foreign ships were not allowed to dock. Large gatherings of people, such as markets and festivals, were cancelled. If people came down with the plague, they were not allowed to leave the house, and their street might even be blocked off. When people died of the plague, their clothes were burned and their bodies were buried outside the city walls. Such quarantine measures did help to limit the disease's spread to uninfected areas.

Measures to improve public health also included keeping streets and waterways cleaner. Many cities hired people to wash and sweep the streets. Lawmakers might forbid dumping certain kinds of waste into the streets or allowing pigs to roam free. Drainage systems began to improve, and laws were passed to limit water pollution. In Nuremberg, for example, rubbish could be dumped into the Pegnitz River only at certain places downstream from the city. The bodies of dead animals were not to be thrown into the river at all, but buried in a field outside the walls.

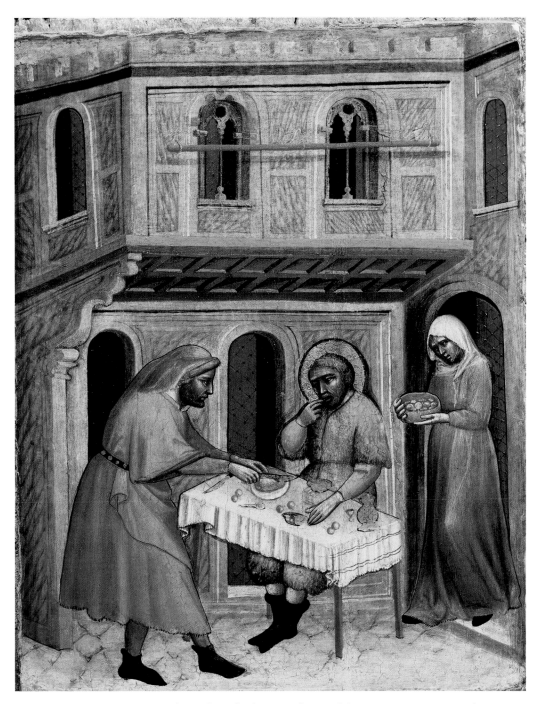

A poor man receives a good meal in the home of a wealthy citizen. Many people in Renaissance cities had to depend on charity or go hungry.

One of the most important urban improvements was care for the poor. By the end of the Renaissance, there were cities with numerous charities that looked after the sick, raised orphans, gave dowries to poor girls, educated underprivileged children, sheltered battered women, fed and housed widows, and more. These institutions might be run by religious organizations or by city governments. There was often much involvement from private citizens, who donated money or helped run the charities. Some of the hospitals, orphanages, and shelters in cities such as Venice would be admired even today.

The people who supported charity in Renaissance cities were expressing care for their towns and for their fellow citizens. They had faith in the human spirit and hope for the future. Their spirit lives on, for in spite of the challenges, the great Renaissance cities survived, and many continued to thrive. Today the achievements of the Renaissance still inspire us and enrich our world.

The Countryside

One

A CHANGING
WAY OF LIFE

During the time we call the Renaissance, 80 to 90 percent of Europeans lived in the country and worked at farming and related jobs. In many ways, their lives went on just as they had done for centuries. The average peasant did not care much about the rebirth of ancient learning or new artistic techniques. Everyday concerns about crops, livestock, and the weather were more important.

Still, country dwellers were more and more affected by the historic changes taking place. For instance, by the 1500s printing presses were turning out inexpensive pamphlets and broadsides. These could include anything from ballads and popular stories to news of overseas discoveries to religious tracts. Traveling peddlers sold these publications at country fairs and the like. Most places had at least one literate person who was willing to read them aloud to other villagers. In many areas village schools were opened, and more country children learned to read than ever before. In England, for example, by 1600 roughly one-third of the nation's males were able to read.

A wealthy couple (in black, on the right) *pay a charitable visit to a busy farmhouse where several generations of a family are living and working together.*

The Reformation was another cause of increasing literacy. The version of the Bible used by the Catholic Church was in Latin, which most people did not understand. Protestants believed that the Bible should be translated into the languages spoken by people in their everyday lives so that all Christians could read the Bible for themselves. Thanks to the printing press and the Reformers, affordable Bibles began to appear in German, French, English, and other languages. This gave ordinary people, especially in Protestant communities, another strong reason to learn to read. Reformers often set up schools to teach them.

Some of the Reformation's effects were less beneficial. The new religious movement sparked wars and other violence that often harmed country communities. In territories that became Protestant, convents and monasteries were closed down. Many peasant communities had depended on these institutions not only for religious guidance but also for medical care, poor relief, and other social services. In addition, numerous country families had rented their land from some of these religious communities for generations. Now convent and monastery lands were taken over by the government or put up for sale.

Farmers who were already fairly prosperous were able to increase their holdings and enjoy a rising standard of living. The average peasant, however, could not afford to buy much land, so wealthy nobles, merchants, lawyers, and the like acquired more and more property. These landowners rented out parcels of land, but there was only a limited amount available to tenants, and rents were high. In addition, birth rates were increasing and the population was growing. The Renaissance "baby boom" led to lower wages and higher prices for food, land, and other resources. Even as life improved for the "middling sort," for poor peasants the Renaissance was a very hard time indeed.

COUNTRY AND CITY

Numerous people left the countryside and moved to the city to try to improve their lives. Others traveled to nearby towns fairly often to attend fairs and markets. Most Renaissance cities had a very close relationship with the surrounding countryside. Many townspeople even left their homes every workday to labor on farms outside the city walls.

Urban areas depended on the country for basic food supplies. Hundreds of peasants might come to a city on market day, bringing fruits, vegetables, eggs, cheeses, and other farm products to sell. Grain was brought into cities by the cartload, cattle were driven to the butchers, and wool was delivered to cloth manufacturers. In return for such products, peasants

A well-off townsman buys a bull from a peasant (in blue jacket), who seems reluctant to let the animal go for just the few coins he's been handed.

received money to pay their rent or perhaps to buy a few things that they could not make or grow themselves.

Many cities ruled the country areas around them. If peasants had legal problems, they had to go into the city to appear in court, pay fines, and so on. For example, Nuremberg, Germany, had a Peasant Court, which was held for three hours every Saturday afternoon. One of Nuremberg's legal advisers explained, "This Peasant Court has jurisdiction over all controversies arising among the rural people of our Territory." In a few places, peasants who owned their own land could choose someone to represent their interests to the local town government. However, this was rare, and country people usually had little say about the laws, taxes, and government decisions that affected them.

LANDLORDS AND THEIR DEMANDS

There were many different arrangements between peasants and landowners. In much of eastern Europe, most sixteenth-century peasants were serfs, tied to a particular estate or piece of land. Eastern Europe did not have many well-developed urban centers, but it did have large areas where grain and livestock could be raised. These products and other raw materials were in high demand in western Europe. Wealthy nobles became even wealthier by meeting that demand. They bought up huge plots of land and gradually required more payments and services from the peasants living on the land. In Poland, for example, laws in 1520 ordered peasants to work one day a week for their lords. Around 1550 the requirement changed to three days a week, and by 1600 it was six days a week.

Serfdom had been common in much of western Europe during the Middle Ages. It still existed in places, but by the 1400s large numbers of serfs had been able to buy their freedom. Freedom meant that peasants were no longer bound to a lord's land. They were free to move from one village to another, and they could buy and sell land of their own. They were free, too, from the many fees that serfs were required to pay their lords. Nevertheless, tenant farmers—those who rented their land—had some obligations. Along with paying rent, they might have to work a few days a year for the landlord or supply him with various farm products. Farmers were often expected to sell most of their produce to the landlord at low prices. The landlord would then resell the grain, wool, and so on at much higher prices.

In many places landlords owned all of a community's mills, ovens, fish ponds, and woods. A peasant who wanted to grind grain, bake bread, catch fish, or gather firewood had to pay the landlord a fee to do so. Landlords usually allowed no one except themselves and their friends to hunt in the woods they owned. Anyone else caught hunting was guilty of poaching, a crime that was seriously punished. The landlord was often responsible for hearing and judging legal cases on his lands, and kept any fines that had to be paid by offenders.

A baker tends to bread that's still in the oven while customers look over the loaves on the counter. In some places villagers baked their bread themselves, in community ovens owned by a lord. Other villages had bakeries, like this one, where people could buy bread from the local baker.

A Free Village

In the village of Artigat in southern France, as in some other villages, all of the landowners were peasants. Poorer peasants might pay rents to richer ones, but no one owed fees or services to any noble landlord. The people of Artigat were very proud of their freedom, especially since the village just upriver had a lord, and a castle from which he could control the peasants who worked his lands.

In a free village like Artigat, all local affairs were in the hands of the villagers themselves. Larger matters were subject only to the king of France and his representatives. For Artigat, the lowest ranking of the king's agents was his judge in the town of Rieux, several hours away. If a matter had to go to a higher authority, it went to the seneschal, or steward, of Toulouse, the leading city in the region. After that, an appeal could be made to the parliament of Toulouse, but it was a rare case that had to be dealt with at such a high level.

Artigat's local government was headed by three or four consuls, leading villagers chosen yearly by an assembly of the community's men. The judge of Rieux had to approve their selection, but that was all. The consuls, who wore red and white hoods as their badge of office, decided such matters as when to start the winter harvest and how to distribute the common lands. They gave judgments on disturbances of the peace, the use of false weights and measures, minor assaults, and similar cases. When a peasant died without heirs, the consuls handled the auction of his goods. If an orphan needed to be assigned a guardian, the consuls took care of that, too. They often called an assembly of all the village's men to take part in decision making—but women were not summoned to join the assembly unless the consuls were proclaiming a law or order for all the village.

Another way for landlords to make money from the peasantry was by charging tolls for using roads or bridges on their property. Even freeholders, peasants who owned their own land, would have to pay these fees when they used toll roads and bridges. Freeholders, tenant farmers, and landlords alike all had to pay taxes to the government and tithes to the Church. In some areas, roughly 40 percent of a peasant's income went just for taxes, tithes, and various fees.

Two

COUNTRY COMMUNITIES

P easant communities differed from one another largely according to how easy the land was to farm. Mountainous areas, for example, could not support as much farming or as many people as level areas with fertile soil. Another factor was the presence of cities. The region surrounding a large town usually had many peasant communities nearby so that the city and countryside could easily benefit from each other. In places like Scandinavia and Scotland, where there were few cities and much of the land was hard to farm, country people tended to live on isolated family farms or in small clusters of just a few farmsteads. On the other hand, in parts of eastern Europe there were villages of a thousand or more people, all of whom were needed to raise the large quantities of grain or livestock that the lords exported to the west. Elsewhere, a good-sized village might be home to between thirty and fifty families.

TRADITIONAL VILLAGES

In fertile farming areas, such as those in southern England and most of France, many villages followed a pattern that was hundreds of years old. The villagers' homes and gardens clustered together, typically on either side of a wide dirt road. Depending on the size of the village, there could be some smaller roads branching off the main one. A river or stream usually flowed not far from the houses. The water might turn a mill wheel to power machinery that ground grain into flour. Some places had windmills instead of, or in addition to, water-powered mills.

At a little distance from the villagers' homes, the landlord (if there

Near the village center, peasants spend an autumn day butchering pigs so that they will have smoked and salted pork to eat during the winter. In the foreground on the right, two children are playing with an inflated pig bladder, a kind of Renaissance balloon.

The Village Church

Most villages had a church. It was usually built of stone and was sometimes the only stone building in the area. The inside of a country church might be decorated with wall paintings showing scenes from the Bible. There could also be a few statues of Jesus and of some of the saints. There were generally no pews—churchgoers had to stand or bring stools from home. As the sixteenth century progressed, however, some Protestant churches began to have benches for worshippers to sit on.

The church could be used for other purposes besides religious services. It provided the best indoor space for meetings of the village council or assembly. And in England, church towers were often considered the ideal place for beehives. The village cemetery was in the churchyard, which was also used as an outdoor gathering place. When traveling preachers visited, they often preached in the churchyard. Some of these preachers were carrying the new Protestant teachings to the countryside. Peasants who embraced the Reformation sometimes destroyed the religious statues and the altar in their church.

The priest or minister was generally appointed by church authorities. He might be a member of a local family, familiar to the villagers since his boyhood. But even when he was a stranger, he would generally become an active member of the community. He not only led worship services and performed baptisms, marriages, and funerals, but also helped villagers with their problems, giving advice, settling disputes, visiting the sick, and so on. Some country priests did not know how to read and write, but those who did could help villagers with letters, documents, and the like. They might even give peasant children some lessons in reading and writing. Many priests were also landowners, and many enjoyed socializing with the other villagers.

was one) often had a residence. This could be a very grand manor house, surrounded by landscaped gardens and parklands. The lord might also have demesne (dih-MANE) land, acreage that he did not rent to tenants; he hired laborers to farm it for him. In addition to fields, the demesne could include orchards, sheep pens, beehives, stables, and the like. Often the landlord's house and land were enclosed by a high fence or wall.

Three large fields surrounded the village houses. Beyond the fields were woods. The woodland nearest to the village was usually reserved for the landlord's use. In woods farther off, the villagers could gather firewood and forest plants and could let their pigs loose to eat acorns and beechnuts. (If there weren't enough acorns on the ground, swineherds used long wooden poles to knock them out of the trees.) "Waste" areas between the farmland and the woods provided peasants with straw, rushes, ferns, and similar products—useful for thatching roofs, covering dirt floors, and making bedding for farm animals. There were also meadows where hay was grown and a common pasture where villagers could let their animals graze.

Three-Field Farming

The village's three fields were farmed according to a system known as openfield or champaign agriculture. (*Champaign* is from a French word meaning "level open country"—and champaign agriculture was still practiced in parts of France well into the nineteenth century.) Each field was divided into long one-acre or half-acre strips, which were easier to plow than square plots of land. The strips were distributed among the villagers so that every farmer had some land in each field. A farmer's strips were also scattered through each field, instead of being right next to one another. In this way everyone had some of the best land, some of the worst land, and some of middle quality. To make the division of land even fairer, many village councils redistributed the strips every year or every few years. Often the strips were assigned by lottery.

The hay meadow was a busy place in the summertime, and many people worked together to cut and gather the hay. Breaks for food, drink, and rest were also good times to socialize.

One field would be planted in fall, one in spring, and one left fallow for the whole year. The next year the fallow field would be planted, and one of the other fields would lie fallow. This was a common form of crop rotation. In some places, instead of having a fall planting and a spring planting, farmers seeded the fields with two different crops. For instance, wheat or rye might grow in one field, while the other had oats, barley, or peas.

Another variation, becoming more common in Italy in the 1500s, was to plant alfalfa or clover in the third field instead of letting it lie fallow. This had been a common practice in Spain for a long time. Many Italian estate owners were influenced not only by the Spanish example but also by new translations of ancient Roman books about agriculture. These writings taught landlords that alfalfa and similar plants not only provided food for livestock but also enriched the soil.

SHEEP AND HEDGES

During the Renaissance, wool was big business. All over Europe the demand for wool was growing, and landowners in some places could make huge profits by raising sheep. This was especially true in England, which produced some of the very finest wool. By 1500, large amounts of land were being converted from raising crops to raising sheep. If a lord switched to sheep farming on his demesne, most of his laborers were put out of work. It took a fairly large number of people to work the fields, but only a few shepherds to take care of sheep. Landlords might also evict their tenants and turn the fields into sheep pastures. Many unemployed farmworkers ended up moving to London and other cities to look for work. Too often, the only way they could support themselves was by begging. The tremendous growth and impact of English sheep farming prompted one writer in 1598 to compose this bitter verse:

> Sheep have eat up our meadows and our downs,
> Our corn,* our wood, whole villages and towns.   [grain]
> Yea, they have eat up many wealthy men,
> Besides widows and orphan childeren,
> Besides our statutes and our iron laws
> Which they have swallowed down into their maws.*   [stomachs]

When fields were converted to sheep pastures, landlords usually enclosed the land with walls or hedges. The practice of enclosure also came to affect crop growing in many areas. In central England, for instance, champaign agriculture was being replaced by what was called farming "in several." Landlords, investors from the cities, and even prosperous peasants

Sheepshearing in the early sixteenth century. This painting, by Simon Bening, comes from a splendid manuscript that was made for a noble family.

In a Land of Grapes and Olives

In the northern Italian region of Tuscany only a few isolated areas had traditional villages with fields shared among different peasant families. Instead, by 1400 the countryside was mostly a patchwork of plots of land called *poderi*. Each *podere* was farmed by a single family, who were sharecroppers. The land was actually owned by someone else, who might live in a villa on the *podere*, or in Florence or another city.

The sharecroppers kept half of what they raised and gave the other half to the landowner. A sharecropper's home was usually in the middle of the *podere*, surrounded by fields, vineyards, olive groves, pastures, and woods. Sharecroppers on the *poderi* tended to live fairly well, though simply. The land they worked was passed down from father to son, so there was a sense of security. They usually produced very profitable products, such as olive oil and wine. This meant they could afford nutritious food, comfortable houses, and good wool and linen for their homemade clothes.

were purchasing more land. As a landowner got control of larger portions of village fields, he was often able to have the strips of farmland redistributed so that all of his land was together in a single plot. Then he enclosed his plot with hedges, and that land was no longer available for common open-field farming. In this way, all of a village's farmland could end up under the ownership and control of a relatively small number of people, with no common land left for anyone else's use. Poor peasants, who could not buy up sizable blocks of land to support themselves, struggled harder than ever to make a living.

Three

HOME SWEET HOME

Country homes could vary tremendously, depending not only on the wealth of the family but also on what resources were available. In places where wood was scarce, houses might be built of stone, brick, or even turf. A common construction method in much of western Europe was wattle and daub. The wattle was a wall of vertical wooden posts with flexible sticks woven between them. This was filled in and plastered on both sides with the daub, a mixture of mud and straw. (In the period shortly after the Renaissance, English settlers built wattle-and-daub houses in Jamestown, Virginia, where reconstructed examples can be seen today.)

In some mountainous areas, roofs were made with wooden shingles, which were weighted with stones so that they would not be blown off by high winds. Where clay was plentiful, roofs might be tiled. A great many country homes had thatched roofs. Straw thatch had many advantages.

A peasant couple cook a meal at their fireside. This picture is part of a larger wall painting made for an Italian palace.

First, straw was easy to come by. Second, the roof straw could provide emergency food for farm animals in hard times. Third, when it was time for a new roof, the old thatch made an excellent fertilizer when it was plowed into the fields. And although new thatch was highly flammable, a thatched roof that had been exposed to many rains and snowfalls was surprisingly fire resistant.

Peasants could not build new houses or repair old ones without permission from the lord or the village council. They had to follow local regulations about getting building materials from quarries or forests. Use of these resources was carefully controlled. In western Germany, for example, five large trees were required to build a house or barn. Ordinances might even specify how thatch should be woven at the rooftop, how wall planks should be arranged, or how the clay should be mixed for wattle-and-daub construction. Approval was also needed for digging wells, building walls, and the like.

MAGNIFICENT MANORS

Wealthy landowners and lords often had large, luxurious country houses. There was no standard design, but a modest English manor house typically had a central great hall with a two-story wing on each side. In front of the house was a courtyard, entered through a gatehouse. Along the sides of this forecourt were stables, barns, and storage buildings. Behind the house, arranged around another courtyard, were buildings for baking, brewing ale, making cheese and butter, and doing laundry. The whole complex was sometimes surrounded by a moat. The house's toilets emptied into the moat, but people still fished in it and let their horses drink from it.

Inside the house, the great hall had a huge fireplace, lofty ceiling, and walls covered with tapestries and wood paneling. (These houses tended to be chilly. Tapestries, besides being decorative, helped cut down on drafts.) High up on one wall might be a minstrels' gallery, a balcony where musicians played to entertain the lord's family and their guests on special occasions. On an average day, however, the lord and his family dined privately in a parlor on the ground floor of one wing of the house. A stairway led from the parlor to a solar, a well-furnished room with several windows. It could be used as a living room, a study, or a place for the women of the family to work on their sewing and embroidery. The other wing of the house had a pantry and kitchen on the ground floor and bedrooms above. There might also be a chapel where the family and servants attended worship services, especially if the manor house was a good distance from the nearest church.

This villa, with its splendid gardens, was owned by the Medici family, who ruled Florence, Italy, during the Renaissance. It was used as a hunting lodge and country getaway.

Even grander were some of the country villas built for nobles or wealthy merchant-bankers in Italy. Some of these villas were at the center of large farming estates, where rents from tenants and sales of farm products were landowners' main sources of income. Other villas were more like "weekend getaways" for wealthy city dwellers who enjoyed having a break from their busy urban lives. The most magnificent villas were designed by noted architects, who were often influenced by ancient Greek and Roman architecture. For instance, several notable villas designed by Andrea Palladio, in the region around Venice, had entryways that looked very much like the facades of ancient temples. In other villas, Greek and Roman influence was obvious in the use of columns, rows of arches, and courtyard fountains and statues. Many Italian country homes were decorated, inside and out, with frescoes illustrating family history or scenes from mythology.

HOMES FOR THE "MIDDLING SORT"

Well-off peasants did not live in the grandeur of lords, but they were fairly comfortable. For example, Francis Drake came from a prosperous peasant family in southern England. (He later became the first Englishman to sail around the world, and a great favorite at Queen Elizabeth I's court.) The Drake farm was about a mile away from a town called Tavistock. When Drake was born in 1540, his family probably had more than a hundred acres of land. The property included a house, barns and stables, a building for brewing ale, sheep pens and pigsties, orchards, gardens, meadows, and woods, as well as fields for crop growing.

In Drake's family, the house and farm buildings were arranged along the sides of a narrow courtyard. The house, built of stone, was a longhouse, a type common in sixteenth-century England. A single fireplace and chimney divided the inside of the house into two areas. One was for farm animals.

Two travelers are given rest and refreshment outside the home of prosperous French peasants. The "middling sort" could afford to be generous, while poor peasant families had hardly enough food, drink, and shelter for themselves.

It probably had a stone floor and a drainage channel in the center, to make it easier to clean up after the animals. Keeping them inside, especially in the winter, helped protect them from the elements and from thieves, and their body heat contributed to the house's warmth. (Unfortunately, the animals' presence also made the house a good deal smellier!)

The fireplace, the only source of heat, faced the house's other section, the main living area. The family had a fire even in warm weather, because all cooking was done at the fireplace. Next to the fireplace there was a stairway that went up into a one- or two-room loft. The loft was used for storage and for sleeping. People also slept in the main living area below, but there were no separate bedrooms. The living area was one large room, perhaps fifteen feet square, with simple furniture.

The mother of William Shakespeare, the great English writer, also came from a well-to-do farm family. When her father died, she inherited his hundred acres, his house and barn (filled with stored wheat and barley), and numerous farm animals. The house was well furnished with oak furniture, copper and brass pans, and eleven cloth wall hangings, which were painted with scenes from Bible stories and Roman mythology.

COUNTRY COTTAGES

The majority of peasants lived in one- or two-room cottages, sometimes hardly better than huts. Many had no chimneys, only a gap in the roof to allow smoke to escape. While prosperous homes often had wood, tile, or stone floors, the houses of poorer country folk had floors of hard-packed dirt. People covered the ground with loose straw or rushes, sometimes with herbs and flowers mixed in.

Poor families had little furniture. They might not even have beds, only straw-stuffed mattresses that they laid out on the floor when it was

A Good Night's Sleep

In 1587 William Harrison wrote a *Description of England*. In it he remarked, "There are old men yet dwelling in the village where I remain, which have noted three things to be marvellously altered in England within their sound remembrance." One of these marvelous changes was "the great amendment (although not general) of lodging"—the improvement that many (but not all) people were enjoying in their sleeping conditions:

> [F]or, said they, our fathers (yea, and we ourselves also) have lain full oft upon straw pallets, covered only with a sheet, under coverlets made of . . . [coarse material]. . . , and a good round log under our heads instead of a bolster or pillow. If it were so that our fathers or the goodman of the house had within seven years after his marriage purchased a mattress or flockbed, and thereto a sack of chaff to rest his head upon, he thought himself to be as well lodged as the lord of the town . . . so well were they contented. Pillows, said they, were thought meet only for women in childbed. As for servants, if they had any sheet above them, it was well, for seldom had they any under their bodies, to keep them from the pricking straws that ran oft through the canvas of the pallet, and razed their hardened hides.

time to go to sleep. They sat on stools, benches, or the ground. Some people had permanent tables, but others just laid a board across two supports when they needed a table. Some had to make do with even less, setting out their main meal on a single platter balanced on a stool. Plates and dishes were made out of wood for the poor, pewter for the better-off.

THE DARK AND DIRTY SIDE OF LIFE

In manor, villa, longhouse, or cottage, there were some conditions shared by all: There was no electricity and no indoor plumbing. Without electricity, there were not many choices for lighting. During the day, light came from the fire and from a few windows, which could be shuttered at night. Well-to-do people had glass in their windows. Others had to make do with oiled paper or perhaps animal skin. In some parts of the English countryside, wicker or oak-slat lattices were set into the windows. During the night, oil lamps were available in some places. Candles, especially beeswax ones, were expensive, so only better-off people could afford to use them much. They were sometimes placed inside lanterns to protect the flame. Generally people had to make do with firelight and perhaps moonlight shining through the windows. Most of the time peasants just went to bed when it got dark.

The lack of indoor plumbing affected people in many ways. Laundry usually had to be washed in a nearby stream or river. This was a time-consuming job, so it was usually done only one or two times a month. When water was needed for cooking, drinking, cleaning, or other household uses, it had to be hauled from the river or stream or drawn from a well. Some households had their own well. In other places, everyone might have to share one or two village wells. If hot water was needed, it had to be heated in a pot or kettle over the fire.

Without indoor plumbing and hot water heaters, a bath was a major undertaking. Well-off people might own barrel-like wooden bathtubs, and

Peasant Food

Here is a simple meal you can enjoy today that is similar to what a French peasant might have eaten during the Renaissance:

Vegetable broth or bouillon: Make according to the directions on the can or package. When it is heated, add some fresh or frozen peas and carrots (cut up or sliced) and let them cook for a few minutes in the liquid.

Salad: If you have a garden, you can pick your own lettuces and herbs. Otherwise use a bag of fresh spring or baby salad greens. If you want to, add some fresh herbs, such as thyme, savory, marjoram, tarragon, or rosemary. Use a simple dressing of oil and vinegar (the French poet Pierre Ronsard recommended walnut oil and red wine vinegar for country salads).

Bread: To eat like a prosperous peasant, you could buy a loaf of French bread. Whole wheat or multigrain bread, from a bakery or baked at home, would be closest to what most people ate. Or you could have unsweetened cornbread—after the Spanish brought maize from the Americas, peasants in some parts of France (and much of northern Italy) commonly ate cornmeal cakes instead of wheat bread.

Cheese: Chèvre (goat cheese) and Brie are types of cheese that were often eaten in the French countryside. Swiss cheese, cream cheese, and Gouda are similar to other kinds of cheese made during the Renaissance.

Cider: In much of France, wine was the most common drink for people of all ages and all classes. But the region of Normandy in northern France was famous for its orchards and for its delicious apple and pear ciders.

Bon appétit!

might use them about once a week. Most country dwellers, though, seem to have made do with a sponge bath now and then, at least in summer. During the winter in much of Europe, it was too cold to consider bathing. But people generally did wash their faces and hands regularly and rubbed their teeth clean with bits of cloth.

There were no flush toilets, of course. Manor houses often had indoor privies that emptied into a moat, ditch, or cesspit. At the average peasant's home, there was an outhouse or two in the yard behind the house. Rich and poor country dwellers alike also used chamber pots, especially at night or in bad weather. These were later emptied outdoors.

four

COUNTRY FOLKS

S ometimes today we think of a village in "old times" as being a
place where everyone was basically the same. Of course villagers
had many shared concerns, and community spirit was especially
strong where land was farmed in common. But there were also great differences between rich and poor in Renaissance villages. These differences
could lead to resentment, jealousy, and competition. Landlords and rich
peasants often took advantage of the poor, and village society was always
dominated by the wealthier and more powerful members of the community.

LANDLORDS AND THEIR AGENTS

The wealthy Italian merchants and bankers who owned rural villas usually
spent most of their time in the nearby city, attending to business. Every so
often they made the short trip out to the country to spend a few days at

A northern Italian landowner fingers his money bag as he listens to the concerns of one of his tenants. The man behind the tenant is probably the lord's bailiff or steward.

their villas. There they could take long, peaceful walks alone in their gardens, or they could entertain friends and enjoy conversation, music, banquets, and the like. They were not very concerned with farming or other country matters, although such subjects might occasionally crop up in conversation.

City-dwelling landowners and those who spent most of their time at court were rarely seen by their tenants. But peasants were very familiar with some of the landlord's employees. There was usually a steward who managed the lord's demesne. He could also be the person in charge of dealing with the tenants for the lord. On behalf of the lord, the steward might judge legal cases that arose among villagers. (Serious cases, however, generally had to be handled by royal, not local, authorities.) Sometimes the steward was the lord's rent collector, too. Otherwise another employee, often called a bailiff, handled this unpopular job.

COUNTRY GENTLEMEN

On small or middle-sized estates, at least in some areas, the lord often took an active interest in farming his lands. This was especially true of much of the lower nobility in France during the sixteenth century. These lords felt a true attachment to their estates, which had been handed down through their families for generations. They felt responsible for taking care not only of their land but also of the people who lived on it. Such landowners knew their tenants and the other villagers personally and frequently socialized with them. They were ready with advice, medicinal herbs from their gardens, and other assistance for the peasants who depended on them.

A country gentleman of this sort led a very active life. He supervised a large number of farmworkers and handled rents and other matters with his tenants. He arranged for the sale of surplus grain and other products, and inspected the health of animals before they were sold at market. He patrolled his lands to make sure that fences and walls were in good repair, that hedges had no breaks, and that irrigation or drainage ditches were not blocked. He planned out gardens and decided what crops to plant and when to plant them. The landowner who personally ran his estate knew exactly when it was the right time to do all the necessary farm tasks, and he knew the best way to do them. If he was away at war or for some other reason, his wife often managed the estate until he returned.

Some country gentlemen even enjoyed doing farmwork themselves. Noël du Fail, a minor nobleman, was this kind of gentleman farmer. He was also an author, and described his pleasure in working and living on the land:

> *In the orchard you'll find me at work with my billhook and pruning hook, my sleeves rolled back, cutting, trimming, and pruning my young bushes according to the moon. . . . In the*

In a carefully tended orchard, farmworkers cut and rake the grass for hay.

garden, creating order according to my plan, straightening up the square of the paths, training this way and that the flowers and roots . . . and getting mad with the moles and voles which do me so much harm, and sowing various and strange seeds; mixing and blending the warm earth with the cold, watering the dry parts, forcing the late fruits, and controlling by knowing tricks, commonly ignored, the effects and results of nature. In the woods, I am deepening my ditches, aligning my walks, and meanwhile listening to a hundred bird songs and getting my workmen to recount a raft of rustic tales. By the streams, amused and solitary on the bank, I fish with a line. . . . Sometimes, too, with a leash of greyhounds and eight running dogs, I shall be out hunting foxes, roebuck, or hares, without knocking down or damaging the laborers' wheat, as do some breakers of the law and common justice.

Shakespeare lived in both London and Stratford-on-Avon and seems to have been equally at home in both.

Mislead night wanderers, laughing at their harm?
Those that "hobgoblin" call you, and "sweet puck,"
You do their work, and they shall have good luck.
Are you not he?

ROBIN: Thou speak'st aright;
I am that merry wanderer of the night.
I jest to Oberon,* and make him smile   [the king of the fairies]
When I a fat and bean-fed horse beguile,
Neighing in likeness of a filly foal;
And sometime lurk I in a gossip's* bowl   [old woman's]
In very likeness of a roasted crab*,   [crabapple]
And when she drinks, against her lips I bob,
And on her withered dewlap* pour the ale.   [loose skin on the neck]
The wisest aunt telling the saddest tale
Sometime for three-foot stool mistaketh me;
Then slip I from her bum. Down topples she,
And "tailor" cries, and falls into a cough,
Then the whole choir* hold their hips, and laugh,   [group]
And waxen* in their mirth, and sneeze, and swear   [increase]
A merrier hour was never wasted there.

—Act II, Scene 1

PEASANTS RICH AND POOR

It took twenty to forty acres for a peasant to produce enough food to feed a family and pay rents, taxes, and tithes. At the higher end of this range, peasants might even have a little surplus that they could sell at a market. If they earned enough money through such sales, they could rent or purchase more land and hire laborers to help them work it. The more land peasants had, the more surplus they could produce—this was nearly the only way for a peasant family to prosper. Some families did become quite well-off by building up their landholdings. Such success was easiest to achieve when peasants could own their own land instead of having to pay rents, which were always rising. In most areas the number of families farming a hundred or more acres was fairly low—perhaps only two or three out of a village of some sixty households.

Families with only twenty or so acres just managed to get by, so long as crops were good. A bad harvest, though, could quickly plunge them into poverty. It was even worse for those with less land. They simply could not raise enough to support themselves. These peasants had to work as laborers for others or find other ways to supplement their incomes. They had little hope of improving their situation. They could not afford to eat any of their pigs, chickens, or eggs, or any of the good fruit that grew on the trees in their gardens. All such products had to be sold just so that these families could pay their rents.

Some of the poorest peasants had only a cottage and garden. As William Harrison wrote in his *Description of England* (1587), "a poor man . . . thinketh himself very friendly dealt withal if he may have an acre of ground assigned unto him whereon to keep a cow, or wherein to set cabbages, radishes, parsnips, carrots, melons, pompions [pumpkins] or suchlike stuff, by which he and his poor household liveth as by their principal food, sith [since] they can do no better." Poor peasants often went to work for rich ones and sometimes borrowed money from them so that they could buy food.

No matter how hard they worked, some peasants still could not make ends meet. They might end up wandering from village to village, surviving

Tax collectors, such as these two men, were almost universally disliked. Many peasants barely managed to produce enough to feed themselves and pay their rents and taxes.

by doing odd jobs, begging, scavenging, stealing, or a combination of these. If they went to a city, they might be lucky enough to find work or to get other help from one of the charitable organizations that many urban communities supported. Unfortunately, poverty, hunger, and homelessness were problems as difficult to solve in the Renaissance as they are now.

WORK, WORK, WORK

Renaissance peasants worked from sunup till sundown, taking advantage of every hour of daylight. The whole family worked, too, except for very young children. Everyone's labor was absolutely necessary for the family to be able to survive. In general, men did the work out in the fields and women worked in and around the house and garden. But women could and did work in the fields, especially at haymaking and harvest time, when every hand was needed.

THE YEAR'S PATTERN

Much farmwork was determined by the time of year and the weather, so the work varied depending on the climate and other conditions in different regions of Europe. For example, many French and Italian peasants tended vineyards, and their activities included the various stages of growing grapes

Harvesting grapes in Italy. The woman on the left has tucked up her long skirts so that she can easily climb the ladder to reach grapes on a vine that has been trained to grow up a tree. Down the hill a large vineyard stretches into the distance.

and making wine. English peasants might be involved in producing cider, since apple trees were plentiful in much of England. Southern Europeans were often able to plant and harvest many weeks earlier than northern Europeans because of the warmer climate. But despite the differences, peasants everywhere followed similar yearly patterns.

Every month had its own labors. January was generally the time for pruning vines and fruit trees, making sure all the farm tools were in good repair, and starting to turn the soil in the gardens and in the fields that would be planted in spring. Some of these labors continued into February, which was also the month for sorting seeds and cleaning out beehives and henhouses. Sheep began to give birth to lambs in February, so shepherds became very busy tending their flocks, and in some places farmwives milked the ewes and made sheep's milk cheese.

The main task in March was to get the fields and gardens planted. Women and children also gathered fresh spring greens, such as violet and dandelion leaves, to make nutritious salads. In April, fields and gardens needed to be weeded, and fruit trees could be planted. May was the month for sheepshearing, making cheese and butter, picking strawberries, watering young trees, and more weeding. In parts of France and Italy, peasants collected silkworm cocoons from mulberry trees in May.

Hay making was June's big job. The hay could only be cut on sunny days (giving us the proverb "Make hay while the sun shines"), so that it could be spread out on the meadows to dry. Then it was gathered into haystacks or loaded into carts to be taken to the barns for storage. Other June tasks were cleaning the threshing floor (where harvested grain would be separated from stalks and seed coverings), harvesting barley, and picking rose petals and herbs to make rose water, medicines, and other products.

In July peasants could begin to harvest the wheat that had been sown the previous fall. They also removed bad fruit from trees so that the remaining fruit would ripen better, and they fertilized grapevines and fruit trees with manure. Harvesting continued in August—along with the grain, melons and cucumbers were now ripe. In France peasants also harvested flax (for making linen) and hemp (for making rope), and in the vineyards they cut away leaves that shaded the ripening grapes from the sun.

September was the month to sow the fall planting of wheat, rye, or other grains. Threshing, begun in July or August, continued. Apples, grapes, and walnuts were ready to be picked. Grain, vegetable, and fruit seeds were saved for the next spring planting, and straw was gathered for thatching. Swineherds drove pigs into the woods to eat acorns, while other people went to the woods to start gathering extra firewood for the coming winter. Many farm animals were now taken to the butcher or sold at the market.

Harvesting grain was August's big job in much of Europe. In this painting by Simon Bening, a woman ties up sheaves of harvested wheat as two men with sickles continue to cut more grain. In the background a heavily laden cart carries bound sheaves away to a barn.

In October, people harvested honey and beeswax from the beehives and gathered flexible twigs, vines, and other materials for making baskets. In grape-growing areas, this was also the month for wine making. November was the time to carry out final preparations for winter. In Italy and France, it was also the month for pressing olives to make olive oil. Then, in December, farm families settled down to making baskets and other utensils, making or mending tools, spinning and weaving, and other indoor tasks.

MORE WAYS TO MAKE A LIVING

It was very common for villagers to do other work along with, or even instead of, farmwork. A great many peasants, especially women, did spinning and weaving in their homes for cloth manufacturers in the towns. English peasant women often brewed and sold ale, and French and Italian peasants might sell wine. Women sometimes baked extra bread to sell to their neighbors, too. Men made extra money by hauling goods in their carts.

Peasant women were often the ones who took eggs, cheeses, and other produce to sell at town markets. Some prosperous peasants were able to engage in selling on a larger scale. They became rural merchants, dealing in grain, wool, and perhaps wine, which they sold in nearby villages and towns. Well-to-do peasants could also earn money by loaning small sums—to be repaid with interest—to their less fortunate neighbors. Some peasants rented their extra horses or oxen to others.

Most villages had at least a few craftspeople or tradespeople—a blacksmith, a carpenter, a shoemaker, a dressmaker, a miller, for example. Sometimes there was also a notary, a man who could read and write documents and draw up contracts for the villagers. In areas where there was a lot of clay, some villagers manufactured tiles and bricks.

Another important job carried on in the countryside was mining. For instance, there were coal mines in northern England and tin mines in southwestern England. In Germany and Hungary there were rich veins of

In a Dutch market around 1560, two peasants from the countryside prepare to sell some of their chickens and eggs. The woman also has a couple of loaves of bread, and the man has a number of small birds, which he probably snared in the hedges or woods near his farm.

gold, silver, copper, iron, and lead. However, miners were often poorly paid, and their working conditions were uncomfortable and dangerous. In compensation, miners might be exempt from serving in the military or paying certain taxes. All the same, peasant men were less and less willing to work as miners. In some areas, working in the mines became a punishment for criminals.

Peasants who lived near a river or the ocean often earned part of their livelihood from fishing. In the Basque country of southwestern France and northwestern Spain, for example, there was a tradition of long-distance

Sailors and Soldiers

The Renaissance's voyages of exploration led to increasing seaborne trade in many nations and to the growth of naval forces to protect overseas shipping. Boys and men in coastal areas might have the opportunity to go to sea instead of farming. As a boy, Francis Drake, for example, was sent from his family's farm to be educated in the home of his seafaring relative John Hawkins. By the time he was in his teens, Drake was sailing with Hawkins and his sons to ports in France, Spain, and the Netherlands. The Hawkins family were fairly successful merchants, but they also engaged in piracy from time to time. This was not an unusual career path for sixteenth-century men who went to sea.

Some male peasants became soldiers. Renaissance rulers were constantly increasing the size of their armies. Before 1500 a typical army was made up of between 10,000 and 30,000 men; in 1570 the number was as high as 85,000. Commanders were generally nobles or well-born gentlemen, but the common soldiers were drawn from among poor peasants and townsmen. Some were recruited by force, or were obligated to provide military service to their lord. Other men enlisted voluntarily, since they might not have any other way to make a living—or they might simply crave adventure. Many of these became mercenaries, soldiers for hire, who would fight in any army that paid them decently.

fishing and whaling expeditions. In fact, the Basques were probably fishing for cod off the coast of Canada at least a hundred years before Columbus landed in the Caribbean. But since the Basques could sell salted cod for high prices and they did not want competition, they never told anyone else about the New World and its fertile fishing grounds.

Six

FAMILY LIFE

A typical peasant household included parents, children, and sometimes a few other relatives, such as a widowed parent or unmarried sibling of the husband or wife. Mothers gave birth to an average of five or six children, but often only two or three lived through childhood. Prosperous peasants generally had a few servants, who might also live with the family. Most households had a cat, to keep down rodents, and perhaps a dog or two, to guard the home and livestock. These cats and dogs may often have been treated with affection, but most people probably thought of them more as working farm animals than as pets.

BIRTH AND BABIES

All babies were born at home. Birth was a frightening and dangerous experience because there were not many medical techniques to help out if

This painting of shepherds adoring the newborn Jesus, as described in the Bible, shows how Renaissance babies were often tightly swaddled to keep them feeling warm and secure. Many people also thought that swaddling was necessary to make sure a baby's arms and legs would grow properly.

something went wrong. In fact, few villages had doctors at all. Women in childbirth often had little more than prayers and traditional customs to rely on for help. For example, in the Italian countryside it was common for a husband (who was usually not allowed to be present) to give his wife his cap to wear for good luck during labor.

Fortunately, many peasants had a good knowledge of herbal medicine, and almost every village had at least one experienced midwife. Midwives were usually older women who not only helped deliver babies but also treated women's health problems. Still, no one in Renaissance Europe knew about germs, so no measures were taken to prevent infection. Even with the help of a skilled midwife, many mothers and babies died during or soon after childbirth.

Unlike many upper-class women, peasant mothers nursed their own children, usually for a year or two. (Sometimes, especially if her own baby died, a peasant woman could earn extra money by nursing and taking care of a child from a noble or wealthy city family.) If a mother died, or could not nurse her baby for some other reason, the child was given goat's or cow's milk from a baby bottle made out of a cow's horn.

Mothers had to go back to work within a few days of giving birth. Often they would carry the baby along with them in a cloth sling or similar carrier. Sometimes babies and toddlers were left in the care of an elderly relative or neighbor, or an older sister might be responsible for looking after younger siblings. Sadly, there were times when peasant parents, with heavy work to do in the fields, had to leave babies or young children alone in the cottage. The children had to wait until the end of the long workday to be fed and tended, and in the meantime they risked injury and even death from fires or accidents.

GROWING UP

Almost as soon as children could walk, they started helping with their parents' work. They stood guard in gardens, fields, and orchards, chasing off birds that might eat seeds or crops. They gathered nuts, berries, and herbs in the woods and meadows. Even fairly young children could pull weeds in gardens and scatter feed for the family's chickens. Older children could take more responsibility for tending sheep, cows, geese, and other farm animals. At home they could fetch water from the well, and in the fields they could sow seeds and bind up sheaves of harvested grain.

In some villages, children might have the opportunity to attend school for a couple of years. They would learn basic reading, writing, and

Two schoolteachers work with students individually while the other pupils study their lessons. Schools like this one often taught poor children for free but expected fees for children from well-to-do families.

arithmetic. A few boys, usually from prosperous families, might continue their schooling and eventually even attend a university. Sometimes a village child became an apprentice to a craftsperson and learned a skilled trade.

The majority of peasant children were educated mostly by observing and assisting their parents. Fathers showed their sons how to make and repair tools. Mothers showed their daughters how to spin, cook, and keep house. Children learned to plant and harvest, to prune trees and vines, to handle livestock, and to master countless other skills by working alongside their parents.

During the teenage years, children usually had the same workload as adults. They didn't always stay at home to work, though. In some areas it was customary for teenage boys to leave the village and go up into the mountains to tend flocks of sheep for the summer. In other places, young adult males commonly joined the crews of fishing fleets. Numerous teenagers—especially girls, and especially from poor families—went to work as servants or hired laborers for several years. For many girls, this was the only way that they could save up a dowry, the money they would need to be able to get married.

A Little Goatherd

Thomas Platter, who eventually became a respected printer and educator, was born into a poor peasant family in 1499. They lived high in the Swiss Alps, where weather conditions and the mountainous terrain made life especially hard. When Thomas was six years old, he went to work as a goatherd. He recalled the experience when he wrote his autobiography toward the end of his life:

> *I was so small, that when I opened the stable door and did not jump aside quickly, the goats knocked me down. I once drove my goats up to a ledge, which was one step wide, with nothing but rock below it for over a thousand fathoms. From the ledge, they climbed a rock face covered in tufts of grass. But when I had gone up the grass a small step, I could go no further, and I dared not jump back to the narrow ledge in case I jumped too far and fell over the terrible precipice. I stayed there for a good while, holding on to tufts of grass with both hands, and supported by my big toe on another tuft. I feared that the great vultures who flew below me would carry me away.*

Fortunately, a friend saw Thomas's predicament and came to his rescue. After Thomas had three more years of difficult and frightening experiences, the aunts who raised him decided he was not going to be a success as a goatherd. They arranged for him to go to school instead.

GETTING MARRIED

Most peasants married when they were in their twenties. Occasionally they were much younger. We know of one case in southern France in which the bride may have been only ten, and the groom thirteen or fourteen. This was very unusual and probably happened because both came from very prosperous families, which were eager to be connected by marriage. Such a connection could increase the wealth and importance of both families.

Marriages were normally arranged by the families of the couple. In some places, such as parts of Italy, midwives assisted in this process by acting as matchmakers. Sometimes the groom-to-be might ask his parents to arrange for him to marry a certain girl. Usually both families were from

Dutch peasants celebrate a wedding with a lively outdoor feast accompanied by bagpipe music. The bride is the third woman from the right; the groom is probably the man with the fur-trimmed collar.

the same village or neighboring villages, so the couple probably knew each other at least a little before they became betrothed, or engaged.

An important part of almost every betrothal was the negotiating and signing of the marriage contract. The contract laid out the terms of the bride's dowry, which might be paid all at once or over a period of several years. A typical dowry for a girl from a well-off peasant family was a cash payment and household goods such as pillows, sheets, a bed, and a storage chest. The bride's family might also include a field or vineyard in the dowry and would probably give the young woman a trousseau of two or three dresses in different colors. The groom's family's part of the contract was mainly to specify how the bride would be provided for if her husband died.

In earlier centuries, peasant weddings had often been very informal. But after the Reformation began, both Catholic and Protestant churches came to insist that betrothals be publicly announced and that couples have formal wedding ceremonies in church. After the ceremony, it was common for a procession of villagers to accompany the bride and groom to their home, where the wedding was celebrated with a banquet.

For Better or Worse

The Renaissance concept of marriage did not have much to do with love. Ideally, the husband and wife should be good companions, friendly and respectful to each other, and partners in caring for their family and property. If the couple were in love, or grew to love each other—and many did— that was a bonus.

Still, most people strongly believed that the husband was the head of the family, superior to his wife in every respect. This idea was expressed everywhere from sermons to jokes. If a wife acted superior to her husband, or if their marriage differed from village expectations in other ways, the young men of the village might stage a charivari at their house. This

An Ideal
Country Couple

This song, written by Thomas Campion for a courtly audience, contrasts a wholesome peasant life with the artificialness of life at court. Such idealizations of country living were common in ancient Greek and Roman poetry, and many Renaissance writers carried on this literary tradition.

Jack and Joan

Jack and Joan, they think no ill,
But loving live, and merry still;
Do their weekdays' work, and pray
Devotely on the holy day;
Skip and trip it on the green,
And help to choose the summer queen;
Lash out, at a country feast,
Their silver penny with the best.

Well can they judge of nappy ale,
And tell at large a winter tale;
Climb up to the apple loft,
And turn the crabs* till they be soft. [crabapples]
Tib is all the father's joy,
And little Tom the mother's boy.
All their pleasure is content;
And care, to pay their yearly rent.

Joan can call by name her cows,
And deck her windows with green boughs;
She can wreathes and tuttyes* make, [bouquets]
And trim with plums a bridal cake.
Jack knows what brings gain or loss,
And his long flail can stoutly toss;
Make the hedge, which others break,
And ever thinks what he doth speak.

Now, you courtly dames and knights,
That study only strange delights,
Though you scorn the homespun gray,
And revel in your rich array;
Though your tongues dissemble deep,
And can your heads from danger keep;
Yet, for all your pomp and train,
Securer lives the silly* swain.* [innocent] [country fellow]

custom differed from place to place, but typically the young men blackened their faces, dressed up in women's clothes, sang mocking songs, and banged pots and pans outside the windows. The charivari taunted the couple, called attention to their "abnormal" marriage, and sometimes perhaps embarrassed them into behaving more traditionally.

Husbands were legally entitled to discipline their wives by hitting and even beating them. Communities tended to disapprove of men who beat their wives too often or too severely, and occasionally an abusive husband was taken to court. But an abused wife could not get a divorce—divorce was hardly ever allowed in Europe at this time. If a peasant marriage did not work out, sometimes one of the spouses (usually the husband) would desert the other. Usually, though, people just had to make the best of a bad situation.

Seven

REST AND RECREATION

Although people in the countryside worked long and hard, they still found time for enjoyment. They might pause in their plowing to listen to the birds singing, or gossip with friends while doing the laundry. Almost everywhere in Europe, peasants took Sunday as a day of rest. In some places they were required by law to attend church, but otherwise they were free to do as they wished with their time. Outdoor dances were often held on summer Sundays. There were also holidays when peasants could take a break from work and enjoy special festivities. Market days and fairs gave further opportunities to experience a change from the daily routine of work.

EVERYDAY PLEASURES

Even workdays could have room for some recreation. At times when many villagers were laboring together, such as hay making, jokes and songs made

A group of harvesters take a rest from their work to share a meal and socialize.

the work more pleasant. On the way home from the fields at the end of the day, friends might socialize in the village tavern. Often this was simply the home of someone who had recently brewed a batch of ale, but some villages had regular taverns or inns. Games and sports were popular with both children and adults. Peasants played checkers, chess, and dice, as well as games like blindman's buff. Wrestling, archery, and swimming were some of the favorite sports.

Barley Break, a Renaissance Game

Barley Break was an outdoor game enjoyed by both children and adults in Renaissance England. Like most games of the time, there were many variations. This one is meant to be played by six people.

The six players are broken up into three sets of partners. Players One and Two are stationed at one end of the field or playing area, with Three and Four at the other end. Players Five and Six stand in the middle. Each pair holds hands until One and Two shout "Barley!" and Three and Four yell back, "Break!" Then One and Three run to meet each other, as do Two and Four. Five and Six try to catch at least one of the runners. If someone is caught before meeting his or her new partner, the pair will go into the middle on the next round. For example, if Two, who is running to meet Four, gets caught, then Two and Four go to the middle, while One and Three go to one end and Five and Six go to the other. But if both pairs meet up without anyone being caught, Five and Six will stay in the middle for the next round.

Like many Renaissance games, Barley Break did not have winners and losers, and there was no definite end point to the game. People simply played it for fun, and stopped when they ran out of energy!

An Evening's Entertainment

Noël du Fail wrote a book called *Propos rustiques* ("Rustic Observations") in 1547. In it he lovingly recorded the life of the French countryside of his time. Here he describes a festive village gathering:

> *On feast days our fathers would sooner have died than not gathered all their fold at the house of some villager, for rest and recreation after the week's work. After a drink, they began to chatter freely about the state of the crops and to listen to each other's tales. Father Jean, the late priest of our parish, was at the head of the table, to give honor where honor is due, a trifle pompous, . . . giving some good teaching . . . or conferring with the oldest of the married women, seated near him with her hood thrown back: and gladly they spoke about some herbs for fevers, colic or the grippe. . . .*
>
> *Then someone of the village would produce a rebeck [a musical instrument a bit like a violin] . . . from under his coat, or a flute, on which he played with great skill, and so seduced were they by the gentle sound of his instrument, with a hautboy [an old type of oboe] which was there to support him, that they were constrained forthwith, putting off their coats and smocks, to begin a dance. The old, to give example to the young, and to show they were not bored, had the first try, making two or three turns of the dance without kicking up their feet much or*

Country people enjoyed lively dances, as this painting by Pieter Brueghel the Elder shows.

leaping about. . . . The young people then did their bit . . . and there was not a man there that did not dance with all the girls, except Father Jean, who had to be pressed a little, saying, "Sir, wouldn't you care to dance?" And then, having played at refusing a little, he went to it and outdid them all . . . and this venerable priest said: "Tut; tut; we never felt younger, we should take things as they come, and bad luck to anyone who halts."

and herbs, bound round about with strings, from the top to the bottom, and sometime painted with variable colours, with two or three hundred men, women and children following it with great devotion. And thus being reared up with handkerchiefs and flags hovering on the top, they strew the ground [with flowers] round about, bind green boughs about it, set up summer halls, bowers and arbors hard by it. And then fall they to dance about it.

Villagers often elected a King and Queen of the May to lead the dancing and direct various sports and competitions, such as races and mock sword fights. There might be entertainment by groups of singers and dancers, who went from house to house and even visited neighboring villages. Plays about Robin Hood were a May Day tradition in England.

Morris dancers performing for the local people as well as for a group of nobles out for a country stroll. The hobbyhorse dances behind "Maid Marian," while the fool collects donations from the audience.

Another popular English custom was morris dancing, performed by groups of men accompanied by the music of pipes and drums. The morrismen wore twenty to forty bells tied around each leg and danced in a lively style, with hops and jumps, waving handkerchiefs in their hands. They were usually led by a fool and accompanied by "Maid Marian" (a man dressed in women's clothes) and a "hobbyhorse" (a man costumed as a horse). While the morrismen danced, the fool flirted outrageously with Maid Marian. The hobbyhorse rushed in and out of the audience, teasing the members, who sometimes joined in the dancing.

Another great festival was Harvest Home, celebrating the completion of the grain harvest, usually in August. The harvesters decorated the final cartload of grain with flowers and wove a figure, often called a corn dolly, out of the last-cut stalks of grain. Then the harvest leader, crowned with a flower garland, led the cart to the barn. Men, women, and children rode on the cart or ran alongside it, singing, shouting, and passing the corn dolly from person to person. After the grain was unloaded, it was time for a feast, featuring cakes made from fresh-ground wheat and cups of frumenty, a drink made of boiled milk mixed with wheat and spices. It wasn't long before pipes, drums, and other instruments were brought out and dancing began. As one writer commented, "Oh, 'tis the merry time, wherein honest neighbours make good cheer, and God is glorified in his blessings on the earth."

Eight

HARD TIMES

For a great many peasants, life could be a continual struggle. But there were things that made hard times even harder, such as disease. During the Renaissance there were repeated epidemics of plague and smallpox. Poor sanitation led to frequent outbreaks of cholera and typhus. Since antibiotics and many other medicines were unknown, disease killed many people. Some illnesses were caused by malnutrition, for far too many peasants did not have enough protein, vitamin C, or other nutrients in their diets.

War was waged repeatedly in Renaissance Europe. Armies often devastated the countryside, raiding farms for supplies, trampling crops, burning barns, and attacking villagers. When war threatened, many peasants fled and took refuge inside the walls of nearby cities. Warfare drove some peasants away permanently, leaving fields abandoned for years, until the landlord could find new tenants. Meanwhile the fields became overgrown

Poverty personified as a ragged beggar, a familiar figure to Renaissance people

with weeds and shrubs, making it hard work to clear them again for planting. It could take the countryside a very long time to recover from the ravages of war.

PEASANT PROTESTS

When the land was at peace, harvests plentiful, and rents and taxes reasonable, peasants generally accepted the hardships of their lives. But there were many times when peasant communities were pushed to the limits of their endurance. As a result, hundreds of peasant uprisings occurred during the Renaissance. They happened all over Europe—from Spain to Hungary, from Sweden to Italy. The uprisings ranged from small protests to local riots to the formation of peasant armies.

Revolts were usually sparked because landlords, nobles, or government officials moved to reduce peasants' traditional rights and privileges. Landlords and rulers in parts of Germany, for example, were trying to take away peasants' free status and make them serfs. All over Europe, lords were claiming sole use of more forests, meadows, and waterways—and the fish, game, and other resources found in them. These claims deprived country people of much of the means of survival that they had counted on for generations. Another point of protest was the passage of new laws or judgments that differed from long-standing legal customs. Peasants were also pushed toward rebellion when landlords or rulers demanded rents, labor services, or taxes that seemed unfair or higher than they ought to be. In some areas attacks against churches and monasteries occurred because peasants resented having to pay tithes. Only once in a while did peasant uprisings have any political goals, such as gaining the right for peasants to be represented in government assemblies.

The largest rebellion, which came to be known as the German Peasants' War, took place in the 1520s. One of its inspirations was Martin Luther's message that all souls were equal before God. The peasants interpreted this to mean

Peasants who were disabled by farm accidents or war injuries generally had no way to support themselves except by begging.

that all people were equal on earth, too. But this was not what Martin Luther meant or believed, and he sided with the German rulers against the peasants.

By the time the Peasants' War was over, the movement had spread throughout Germany and into Switzerland, Austria, and France. It may have involved as many as 300,000 people. In addition to peasants, many craftspeople, poor city dwellers, minor nobles, and others took part. The rebels were never united under a common leadership, though. The Peasants' War was, in fact, a series of scattered uprisings rather than a single coordinated campaign.

What Rebels Wanted

In William Shakespeare's play *Henry VI*, *Part 2*, a former sheepshearer and beggar named Jack Cade leads a band of peasants and craftsmen in rebellion against the "scholars, lawyers, courtiers, and gentlemen" who seem to run the kingdom. Cade promises his followers:

> *Be brave, then, for your captain is brave and vows reformation. There shall be in England seven half-penny loaves [of bread] sold for a penny, and the three-hooped pot shall have ten hoops, and I will make it a felony to drink small [weak] beer. All the realm shall be in common [common land], and in Cheapside [a business center in London] shall my palfrey [horse] go to grass. And when I am king, as king I will be . . . there shall be no money. All shall eat and drink on my score, and I will apparel them all in one livery [uniform] that they may agree like brothers, and worship [honor] me their lord.*

> —Act IV, Scene 2

Shakespeare's tragedy *Coriolanus* opens with a protest that has more serious and realistic goals than Jack Cade's. Although *Coriolanus* is set in ancient Rome, the protesters' concerns are true to what the common people of the Renaissance often felt. As the leader of the uprising explains, the poor cannot afford to buy bread, while the rich have storehouses full of grain:

> *We are accounted poor citizens, the patricians [nobles] good. What authority [those in authority] surfeits on [overindulges in] would relieve us. If they would yield us but the superfluity [extra] while it were wholesome we might guess [think] they relieved us humanely, but they think we are too dear [too expensive to take care of]. The leanness that afflicts us, the object of our*

A rich man ignores the pleas of a beggar in this illustration from an English book published in the 1560s.

misery, is as an inventory to particularize their abundance; our sufferance is a gain to them. Let us revenge this with our pikes [pitchforks] ere [before] we become rakes [as thin as rakes]; for the gods know I speak this in hunger for bread, not in thirst for revenge. . . . [The nobles] ne'er cared for us yet: suffer us to famish, and their storehouses crammed with grain; make edicts for usury [moneylending at high interest] to support usurers; repeal daily any wholesome act established against the rich; and provide more piercing statutes daily to chain up and restrain the poor. If the wars eat us not up, they will; and there's all the love they bear us.

—Act I, Scene 1

The movement began peacefully in 1524 with large assemblies of peasants discussing their grievances and staging what we would call protest marches. Pamphlets were even printed and distributed in support of the peasants. But before long, rebel bands were raiding monastery storehouses,

A peasant, armed only with a shovel, makes a desperate attempt to protect his family and farm from an invading army.

pulling down nobles' castles and fortresses, and occupying towns. While some of these actions were orderly and highly organized, others were carried out by unruly mobs. One group of rebels even executed some captured nobles. In spite of this episode, however, it was fairly rare for the rebels to commit violence against people.

Unfortunately, government authorities had no hesitation about using violence. They sent armies of mercenary soldiers to crush the uprisings. In May of 1525, 18,000 rebels were killed in a single encounter—it could not really be called a battle, since the peasants and their allies could offer no real resistance to the professional soldiers. By the time the movement was completely dead, in the summer of 1526, as many as 100,000 people had lost their lives.

The rebels had succeeded in at least one point, however: German peasants remained free from serfdom. There were still few in Europe who believed that every person was "created equal," with "unalienable rights" to "life, liberty and the pursuit of happiness." But in just a few centuries, that idea would be embraced by a new nation in the New World. The peasants' struggles for their rights and freedom helped pave the way.

The Church

CHRISTIAN ROOTS AND BRANCHES

For more than a thousand years, one religion dominated western Europe: the form of Christianity that is generally known as Catholicism. The Catholic Church was a strong institution, providing order and stability to most of Europe after the fall of the Roman Empire in the late fifth century. From its headquarters in Rome, the Church was able to influence politics and society, as well as the religious beliefs of the people. From time to time, the Church's authority was challenged by small groups of people whose views on Christianity differed from official Catholic teachings. Nevertheless, for hundreds of years most Europeans were content to look to the Church to satisfy their spiritual needs.

In the middle of the fourteenth century this began to change. A terrible plague swept through Europe, in most areas wiping out one-third to one-half of the population. This disaster shook the faith of large

For all Renaissance Christians, the heart of their religion was faith in Jesus, who had overcome death and promised eternal life to all who believed in him. The first person to see Jesus after he rose from the dead was his follower Mary Magdalene, who encountered him in the garden outside his tomb.

numbers of plague survivors. Many believed that the plague was a punishment for sin and that the Church had failed to help people overcome sin and its consequences. By the fifteenth century, large numbers of Europeans felt overwhelmed by a sense of human sinfulness, and they had a deep fear of going to hell. For numerous Christians, the Church's traditional teachings and ceremonies did little to help them feel assured of God's forgiveness.

At the same time, many people complained that the Church abused its power and paid more attention to worldly affairs than to matters of the spirit. By the early sixteenth century, a significant number of Europeans were longing for a purer form of Christianity, in which they could relate to God as individuals, without the aid of a Church that they now saw as hopelessly corrupt. They wanted a direct relationship with God, with no priests or saints standing in between. Only in this way, such people felt, could they be sure of salvation—the saving of their souls from eternal punishment for sin.

Inspired by such convictions, the Protestant Reformation began. It started out as a protest against certain practices of the Church. Gradually the protest evolved into an effort to reform the entire religious life of Europe. Protestantism had great appeal to many, largely because its services, hymns, prayers and, especially, the Bible were in the everyday language of the people—German, French, English—rather than Latin, which was used by the Catholic Church. For the first time, average people could read the Bible on their own. Many Europeans, however, remained passionately attached to the traditions of Catholicism. Each side was convinced that it was right. Religious differences resulted in widespread conflict—between husbands and wives, parents and children, rulers and subjects. Violence in the name of religion erupted again and again, ranging from riots to full-scale wars. To the people of the time, their very souls were at stake.

THE STORY OF JESUS

To understand what religious life was like for Renaissance people, we need to start with the beginnings of Christianity. Christianity was (and is) based on faith in one all-powerful, all-knowing God, present everywhere at every time. This same belief was (and is) also held by Jews and Muslims. Christianity, however, taught that the one God was revealed as three "persons," distinct from one another yet completely unified. The three-in-one, or Trinity, was made up of God the Father, God the Son, and God the Holy Spirit. The Son was Jesus Christ, and his life and teachings were the centerpoint of Christianity. His story is told in the Gospels, the first four books of the New Testament of the Bible.

Jesus was a Jew who lived in the kingdom of Judea (an area

The baby Jesus with his mother, Mary, by the great Florentine artist Sandro Botticelli

roughly equivalent to the modern nation of Israel) from around 4 BCE to 30 CE* The Gospels relate that he was sent by God to save humanity from its sins. Jesus' mother was Mary, the wife of a carpenter named Joseph. The Bible describes Jesus' birth and one episode from his childhood, and then picks up his story at about the age of thirty. At this time, Jesus went to his cousin John for baptism, a ceremony in which John symbolically cleansed people of their past sins so that they could begin to live more righteous lives.

For the next three years, Jesus traveled throughout Judea, performing miracles, healing the sick, and teaching. Many of his lessons centered on the power of love: "You shall love your neighbor as yourself" (Matthew 22:39). Jesus also preached the importance of the Golden Rule: "Whatever you wish that men would do to you, do so to them" (Matthew 7:12). He taught that those who believed in him and followed his teachings would achieve salvation and have an eternal life in the presence of God. Jesus attracted a large number of followers, both women and men. Twelve of these followers, the disciples or apostles, were his most devoted students.

Judea was part of the Roman Empire, and some people feared that Jesus was trying to start a rebellion and make himself "King of the Jews." He was arrested and put on trial. Condemned to death by the Romans, he was crucified, or executed by being hung on a cross. Three days later, the Bible says, some of his women followers went to his tomb and found it empty. An angel told them that Jesus had been resurrected—he had risen from the dead. After this, Jesus appeared several times to his followers, promising forgiveness of sins and resurrection to all who believed in him. Then he ascended to heaven to rejoin God the Father.

*Many systems of dating have been used by different cultures throughout history. This series of books uses BCE (Before Common Era) and CE (Common Era) instead of BC (Before Christ) and AD (Anno Domini) out of respect for the diversity of the world's peoples.

Jesus was crucified between two criminals on a hill outside Jerusalem known as Calvary or Golgotha, "place of the skull." His mother and his disciple John stayed with him right up until his death.

THE CHURCH'S GROWTH

After the death of Jesus, his followers continued to spread his teachings. At first most Christians were Jews, who generally felt they were practicing a new form of Judaism. Soon non-Jews also began to embrace the Christian faith. Before long Christianity was an independent religion, practiced throughout the Roman Empire. Still, by the fourth century, only about 10 percent of western Europe's people were Christians, and Christianity had a much lower status than most other religions. But in 313, the Roman emperor Constantine decided to give Christianity equal rights and privileges with other religions. Most of the emperors who came after Constantine were Christians, and they continued to strengthen the Christian church. By the year 400 Christianity was the official religion of the empire.

Christianity also spread beyond the bounds of the Roman Empire. Over the course of several centuries, missionaries traveled to almost every part of Europe. They preached the new faith and established churches and monasteries. Many people were persuaded to convert to Christianity. When a ruler converted, he usually required all of his people to become Christians as well, whether they wanted to or not. In the countryside, though, people often continued many of their traditional practices alongside Christianity. For example, in parts of the British Isles people kept up the ancient practice of lighting bonfires and leaping over them on Midsummer's Eve, simply moving the celebration from the summer solstice (around June 22) to the Feast of Saint John (June 24).

Holy Helpers

The Church grew not only in size, but also in beliefs. As time went on, Catholics honored more and more saints. These were people who had led especially holy lives and, after death, were believed to be able to help

Saint Augustine of Hippo, by Sandro Botticelli. Augustine converted to Christianity in 387 and helped spread the religion in his native North Africa. He was also one of the early Church's most important writers and teachers.

Jesus is baptized in the Jordan River by his cousin John the Baptist. The sacrament of baptism recalled this important event for Christians.

Communion, but members of the congregation did so less frequently, even if they attended church every week or even every day. In order to receive Communion, a person was supposed to be cleansed of sin first. This was done in the sacrament of confession or penance, in which individuals confessed their sins to God through a priest. The priest then assigned a penance for the worshipper to perform in order to atone for the sins. The penance often took the form of saying a certain number of prayers. Some people confessed once a year or more, while others postponed confession until they were dying.

The other sacraments marked certain important events in a person's life. Soon after babies were born, they were welcomed into the Church by the sacrament of baptism. During baptism the child was sprinkled with holy water and blessed in the name of God the Father, the Son, and the Holy Spirit. The parents and godparents pledged to raise the child to live according to the Church's teachings. The sacrament of confirmation, in which the child was anointed with holy oil, made the baptism complete. By the Renaissance, children were typically receiving confirmation around the age of seven.

Most people took part in the sacrament of matrimony, or marriage. But priests, monks, and nuns were not allowed to marry. The sacrament of holy orders was for men who dedicated their lives to serving the Church by joining the priesthood. Every Catholic, however, expected to receive the sacrament of extreme unction. This took place when a person thought to be close to death made a last confession to a priest. The priest forgave the sins and then anointed the person with holy oil in preparation for death.

Two

POWER AND PROTEST

Under the organization of the Catholic Church, all of western Europe was divided into parishes. *Parish* basically means "neighborhood"; a parish could be two or three small villages, a single village, or a section of a large village or town. Every parish had its own priest and its own church and cemetery. A number of parishes were grouped together to form a diocese, which was overseen by a bishop. An archbishop had charge of an archdiocese, a group of dioceses. At the head of the entire Church was the pope, who was also the bishop of Rome.

According to Catholic tradition, the first bishop of Rome was Saint Peter, one of Jesus' twelve apostles. The name *Peter* means "rock." Before Jesus died, he had said to Peter, "On this rock I will build my church. . . . I will give you the keys of the kingdom of heaven" (Matthew 16:18–19). The bishops of Rome came to be regarded as the successors of Saint Peter, and this was one reason for the pope's great authority.

Renaissance popes surrounded themselves with beauty and splendor, and their courts were often centers of art and learning. In this fresco, Pope Sixtus IV (enthroned on the right), appoints the noted scholar Bartolomeo Platina (kneeling) as his palace librarian.

By the eleventh century, the pope was advised by a council called the College of Cardinals. All cardinals were appointed by the pope, who could name any Catholic male to the position. (Like the pope, cardinals held office for life.) It was common for popes to name relatives as cardinals and to grant cardinalships as a way of getting or repaying favors from powerful men. During the Middle Ages and Renaissance it was not necessary for a cardinal to be a priest. Sometimes it was not even necessary for him to be a grown man—a son of Lorenzo de' Medici, the unofficial ruler of Florence, became a cardinal at the age of thirteen. When a pope died, the College of Cardinals elected a new pope. From the 1300s on, all new popes were chosen from among the cardinals.

PRINCELY POPES

Medieval and Renaissance popes were actively involved with politics and other worldly affairs. Beginning in the 750s, the pope ruled Rome and the surrounding area, a region of central Italy known as the Papal States. Some popes were not above scheming or even going to war to increase this territory. For example, in the late fifteenth century the Republic of Venice was expanding south to the border of the Papal States. In 1508 Pope Julius II formed an alliance with France, Spain, and the Holy Roman Empire to destroy the Venetian state. In addi-

tion, the pope excommunicated Venice, decreeing that no one in the city might take part in any of the seven sacraments. (Most Renaissance people dreaded the punishment of excommunication, which they believed endangered their souls. The independent-minded Venetians, however, simply ignored the pope's order and continued to worship as usual.)

Pope Julius II, who personally went to war when necessary to maintain his power, was also an outstanding patron of the arts. This portrait of Julius is by Raphael, one of the Renaissance's greatest painters.

Many Renaissance popes cultivated a princely lifestyle. This was both a matter of personal taste and an effort to show the Church's power. One result was that the popes became enthusiastic patrons of the arts. Some of Italy's greatest artists and architects, among them Michelangelo and Raphael, worked on various papal projects in Rome. Both artists were involved in the construction of Saint Peter's Basilica, the huge church at the heart of the papal court.

A few popes seriously abused their power for personal ends. The most notoriously corrupt pope was Alexander VI (pope from 1492 to 1503). He used his daughter Lucrezia to help him gain more power in Italy by marrying her first to one Italian ruler, and then dissolving her marriage so that she could marry another ruler. He also supported his son Cesare Borgia's conquests of several central Italian cities. Alexander and Cesare developed a murderous reputation for poisoning those who opposed them, including bishops, cardinals, members of Rome's leading families, and Lucrezia's second husband.

Some cardinals, too, seem to have cared very little for their own souls or anyone else's, but most were probably sincere in their religious beliefs. Nevertheless, cardinals tended to be much more worldly during the

Cardinals, like this elegant church-man portrayed by Raphael, were known by their red silk robes.

Neither Catholic nor Protestant

Although the Catholic Church held sway over western Europe, most Europeans east of Poland and Hungary belonged to the Eastern Orthodox Church. The Orthodox Church had split off from the Catholic Church in 1054, largely because the bishops of Greece and Asia Minor did not want to be subject to the pope. There were other disagreements, too, but even in the fifteenth century the two churches were holding meetings to try to overcome their differences and reunite. Few Eastern Orthodox Christians lived in western Europe during the Renaissance, except in Venice and its colonies. Venice, a thriving center of international business, also had many Muslim residents.

Much of eastern Europe during the Renaissance was ruled by the Ottoman Empire, a Muslim state. Some people in the Balkan Peninsula and elsewhere converted to Islam, but most remained Christian. Christianity was tolerated by the Ottoman government, although Christians did have to pay a special tax, and churches were not allowed to ring their bells. Until 1492 there was also a Muslim state in southern Spain, the kingdom of Granada. In that year, however, Granada was conquered by Spanish rulers Ferdinand and Isabella. Seven years later the royal couple decreed that all Muslims must either be baptized as Christians or leave the country.

In 1492 Ferdinand and Isabella had set down the same conditions for Spain's Jews. Not only in Spain, but in most of Europe, Jews were often viewed with suspicion and even hatred. Jewish customs and religious practices set them distinctly apart from the Christian majority. Jews did not accept the divinity of Jesus, and many Christians even blamed the Jewish people for the death of Jesus. There was also resentment against Jews because they often worked as

moneylenders—a practice forbidden to Christians by the Church. (It was, however, one of the few ways in which Jews were legally allowed to earn a living in most European countries.)

The Jews of Spain were given four months to either be baptized or make their preparations for leaving. Around 50,000 Jews were baptized, but more than 100,000 emigrated. Some settled in Portugal, but four years later the Portuguese king also banished all Jews from his realm. In 1498 Nuremberg expelled its entire Jewish population, and other German cities soon did the same. (Jews had not been tolerated in England since the thirteenth century, when they were expelled. They were not allowed to return until the seventeenth century.)

Many banished Jews went to cities in central and eastern Europe, where they were able to build thriving communities. Jews who settled in the Ottoman Empire received the same religious tolerance as Christians there. A great many Jews moved to Venice and Rome. In fact, in Rome—the center of Catholicism—Jews lived in greater freedom and security than almost anywhere else in western Europe during the Renaissance. Unfortunately, even though their lives and property were protected by the pope, they constantly encountered prejudice in many forms. For all of the Renaissance's enlightened learning, it was an age when most people found it very difficult to understand or accept ways that were different from their own.

A Jewish couple read from a sacred text during their celebration of the Passover holiday.

Renaissance than now. Many patronized artists and writers, lived in luxuriously furnished palaces, and enjoyed hosting and attending lavish parties. Cardinals were often very wealthy men, and sometimes ambition for greater power tempted them into corruption. In 1518, for example, a group of cardinals plotted to kill Pope Leo X. Their plans were discovered; Leo forgave some of the cardinals after they made public confessions and paid him large fines, but the ringleaders were stripped of their rank and then executed.

The plots and abuses of power that went on in the papal court and among the cardinals upset many Christians. At lower levels of the Church hierarchy, too, there were practices that caused growing concern. Many bishops were appointed for personal or political reasons and never even visited their dioceses. There were also priests who seldom set foot in their parishes, but gave the care of their churches and congregations to others. Many priests were unqualified for their positions in the first place—for example, they were too young, or were not well educated in the Church's teachings. Priests of all ranks often had unofficial wives and fathered children, even though Church law prohibited priests from having relationships with women. Such inconsistencies fueled a growing dissatisfaction with the Church.

Tickets to Heaven?

One of the pope's spiritual powers was to grant indulgences. An indulgence was a kind of pardon for sins. Many people believed that an indulgence could reduce the time they would spend in purgatory, the place of suffering where the soul went after death to be purified before going to heaven.

Indulgences had been used in different ways over the course of several centuries. For example, a soldier who went on a Crusade was able to get an indulgence that accepted his fighting for the Church as a penance for any sins he had committed. Or an indulgence might be granted to a person

This illustration, from a German book published in 1521, shows the pope signing and selling indulgences.

who was given a difficult penance, such as going on a long pilgrimage, so that he or she could make a donation to the Church or charity instead. People who donated money in return for indulgences were, however, still expected to confess their sins in a prayerful spirit of remorse.

Receiving donations in exchange for indulgences became a way for the Church to raise funds. In 1515 Pope Leo X needed money to complete the building of Saint Peter's Basilica. For this reason he authorized the archbishop of Mainz, Germany, to offer indulgences in return for contributions to the building fund. The archbishop's agents sold the indulgences and raised a large amount of money. But the agents did nothing to encourage buyers to have the proper spirit of penitence. Instead, they sold letters of indulgence that they said pardoned sins—even future sins—and eliminated time in purgatory. These certificate-like documents were sometimes mockingly called "tickets to heaven" by critics. The way the indulgences were sold made it sound to many as if the Church was saying that money was more important than prayer and that people could bribe God to let them into heaven.

The biggest critic of the German indulgence sale was the monk and university professor Martin Luther. In the fall of 1517 he wrote a letter of protest to the archbishop. Along with the letter he sent a list of criticisms of indulgences, hoping to encourage debate on the subject. According to tradition he also nailed this list, the Ninety-five Theses, to a church door, in his hometown of Wittenberg, that functioned as a kind of bulletin board for his university. Luther's protest soon snowballed into a movement that shook most of Europe.

NEW KINDS OF CHRISTIANS: THE PROTESTANTS

Thanks to the printing press, within a month the Ninety-five Theses were being read all over the Holy Roman Empire (centered in what are now Germany and Austria). Already disturbed by the other abuses in the Church, people debated not only the sale of indulgences but also the authority of the pope. Luther himself had not originally questioned the pope's authority but before long he did reject it. In April 1520 he wrote to Pope Leo "I must . . . acknowledge my total abhorrence [hatred] of . . . the Roman court, which neither you nor any man can deny is more corrupt than either Babylon or Sodom [cities described as centers of wickedness in the Bible], and, according to the best of my information, is sunk in the most deplorable and notorious impiety. . . . The fate of the court of Rome is decreed; the wrath of God is upon it."

Luther had other ideas that ran counter to the Church's teachings. In fact, he felt that the Church's teachings did not have any true spiritual authority, unless they were founded on what was written in the Bible. For Luther, scripture was the sole authority. Based on his reading of the New Testament, he came to believe that people could find favor with God only by having faith that Jesus had died for their sins. Good works—attending church, praying to saints, or giving to charity—could not earn God's grace.

As a result of these ideas, Luther recognized only two sacraments, baptism and communion. He also concluded that everyone who truly had

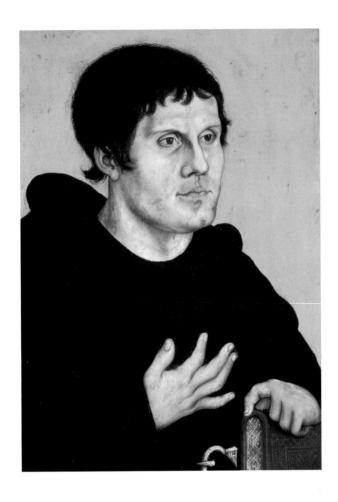

Martin Luther, painted by Lucas Cranach the Elder, a German artist who began the tradition of Protestant religious painting. Luther's gesture here seems to show that his heartfelt faith ultimately rests on the Bible.

faith in Jesus was equal before God. Therefore, there was no need for priests to act as mediators between individuals and God, and there was no special calling for monks and nuns to dedicate themselves to lives of prayer. Instead, all people were responsible for developing their own direct relationship with God, through simple faith in Jesus. To the many Renaissance people who were terrified of going to hell and felt powerless to win salvation, Luther's teachings offered new hope.

In January 1521 the Church excommunicated Luther. A few months later he had to attend a hearing before Holy Roman Emperor Charles V, who did not want religious controversies in his lands. Luther refused to change any of his ideas, and the emperor declared him an outlaw. Luther went into hiding for two years. During this time, he translated the New Testament from the official Latin version into German so that everyone would be able to read scripture for themselves. The ability of any Christian to read and interpret the Bible was to become one of Protestantism's key teachings.

Humanism and Reform

One of the great cultural movements of the Renaissance was humanism, which began as a program to reform higher education. For centuries, education had concentrated on logic and had been based largely on commentaries on the Bible and on a small selection of Greek and Roman works. Beginning in the late fourteenth century, more and more manuscripts of ancient literature and philosophy were becoming available in western Europe. These works—by Plato, Cicero, and others—inspired a number of scholars and teachers to encourage a course of study based on Greek and Roman models of education. The main subjects were those known as the humanities: grammar (or languages), literature, history, philosophy, and rhetoric (the art of persuasive writing and speaking). The Renaissance people who promoted and followed this program came to be known as humanists.

When the humanists studied Greek and Roman literature, they wanted to thoroughly understand the languages that the authors wrote in. They also wanted original sources, not commentaries or summaries, and they wanted the most accurate versions of these sources possible. This humanist concern with language, original sources, and accuracy soon came to influence religious studies. Scholars began to read the Bible and early Church records in a new, more critical way.

In 1440, humanist Lorenzo Valla examined a document known as the Donation of Constantine. It recorded a grant that the Roman emperor Constantine made to the pope, giving him and his successors rule over Italy as well as spiritual authority. Much of the popes' power came from people's acceptance of this document. Valla, however, was able to show that words used in the document could not have been in use during the time of Constantine, in the early fourth century. The Donation was a fake, produced in the eighth century. Valla's

essay about his discovery was not printed until 1517, when German author Ulrich von Hutten came across it and had it published in Germany. In 1520 Martin Luther read this edition of Valla's work. The knowledge that the Donation of Constantine was a fraud helped Luther make up his mind to reject the pope's authority.

Some humanists used their new literary skills to study the Bible. In 1500 the Dutch scholar Erasmus decided to study the original version of the New Testament, which had been written in Greek. As he examined the Greek text, he realized that the Church's official Latin version of the New Testament was full of mistranslations and other mistakes. Erasmus spent several years making a new Latin translation. In 1516 he was finally able to publish this work, which included the Greek text along with his translation. At the same time, he also published a book of notes and comments on the New Testament. With these publications, Erasmus opened a new era of biblical studies. Moreover, he paved the way for the Reformers who would soon be publishing the Bible in German, French, English, and other languages, making the words and teachings of Jesus directly available to more people than ever before.

Humanist studies influenced many churchmen, such as the monk and mathematician Luca Pacioli, who studied and built on the works of ancient mathematicians.

Another important Protestant idea was predestination, which Luther first wrote about in 1525. According to this teaching, whether or not a person would achieve salvation was predestined from birth. In other words, since God knew everything about every person, from the beginning to the end of time, he already knew who was saved from sin and who was not. And since God was all-powerful, he alone was the cause of all human actions. Therefore, human beings had no free will to choose whether they would sin or not, and there was nothing that people could do to guarantee that they would go to heaven. Christians, said Luther and those who followed him, must simply have faith in Jesus and trust in God's grace and mercy.

Spreading the Reform

Luther wrote many pamphlets, books, and letters, which were printed and distributed widely. He also composed popular folksong-like hymns that expressed his faith. While the Church used Latin for all of its writings, Luther used German. The combination of printing and the everyday language of the common people quickly carried Luther's ideas throughout Germany, Austria, and Switzerland.

Among those who embraced Luther's reform were a number of German territorial rulers and independent city governments. In addition to the personal appeal of Protestant beliefs, political and financial considerations were also at work. Many German governments were glad to be free of the pope's authority, which they felt undermined their own power. Breaking away from the Catholic Church also allowed rulers to make great profits by taking over Church property—the duke of Württemberg, for example, doubled his income in this way.

It wasn't long before Protestantism was making waves outside Germany. In Switzerland an influential priest and scholar named Ulrich

Zwingli spread many of Luther's teachings and gave his own version of others. Like Luther, Zwingli rejected the Catholic belief that Jesus was actually present in the bread and wine of Communion. Luther believed that Jesus was still present in spirit. For Zwingli, on the other hand, taking part in Communion was simply a way to remember and express thanks for the sacrifice Jesus had made for humanity. This symbolic view of Communion was taken up by many Protestants who came after Zwingli.

In the 1520s and 1530s, the kings of Sweden and Denmark embraced the Reformation. Lutheranism became the official religion throughout Scandinavia. In 1534 the English king Henry VIII also rejected the authority of the pope, for personal and political reasons. He established the Church of England, with himself at its head. Although Henry disbanded monasteries and confiscated their property, in many ways the Church of England stayed close to Catholicism.

At about the same time, the Frenchman Jean (or John) Calvin was developing another form of Protestantism. He took Luther's ideas about predestination and developed them further, giving predestination a central place in his teachings. For Calvin, everyone who had faith in Christ did so because God had already chosen them to be saved. Believers could therefore feel comforted in knowing that they were predestined for heaven.

Calvin's ideas became very influential among Protestants in France and the Netherlands, although both areas remained under Catholic rule. Some English Protestants, known as Puritans, wanted the English church to follow along the lines taught by Calvin. A Calvinist form of Protestantism did become Scotland's official religion in 1560. With this, over half of Europe had left the Catholic Church.

Three

COMMUNITY LIFE

n Renaissance Europe, there were several kinds of religious communities. Catholicism alone offered a range of options for involvement in religious life. The average person could simply attend church, listening to the priests chant the Mass and joining in on the prayers. A very devout person might decide to join a monastery, a community of men or women who spent most of their time in prayer or good works. Protestantism, on the other hand, did away with monasteries. There was no role for monks or nuns to play in the new belief system.

A PLACE APART

A monastery was supposed to be a place where the cares of the world were put aside so that the residents could devote themselves completely to God. Some monasteries were in the countryside or in lonely places such as forests

The founder of the Dominican order of monks and nuns was Saint Dominic, shown here in a fresco from a Dominican monastery in Florence. The artist was Fra Angelico, who was also a Dominican monk.

or islands. Other religious communities were on the outskirts or even in the middle of cities. Although monasteries were largely self-contained, monks and nuns were not always completely cut off from society—there was usually some interaction with the surrounding community.

The center of a monastery was its cloister, a square or rectangular covered walkway around a garden or open area. Many cloisters were enclosed, with glass windows looking out on the garden. Monks and nuns might spend hours each day in such a cloister, which often had alcoves where they could sit to read, pray, or meditate. From the cloister, monks and nuns could get to the other important monastery rooms and buildings, including the monastery's church. There was also a chapter house, the business center of the monastery. The refectory was the monastery's dining hall.

Fra Angelico's most famous painting, set in a cloister, shows the angel Gabriel telling Mary that she would be the mother of Jesus. The fresco adorned a wall near the dormitory in Fra Angelico's monastery.

Sleeping quarters were in a dormitory. This was usually a corridor or large room divided into small cells, each containing little more than a bed. A "night stair" often led from the dormitory directly to the church so that the residents could easily get to nighttime church services.

Large monasteries might have many other buildings besides those around the cloister. There could be workshops for different crafts, stables for horses, barns, a mill for grinding grain, and guesthouses. Guests entered the monastery through a gatehouse. This was also a place where poor people came to receive food, clothing, and other assistance from the monks or nuns.

Wealthy religious communities frequently owned farms, forests, flocks of sheep, ships, and other property outside the monastery walls. These resources not only supported the monks or nuns and aided the neighboring poor, but also financed the creation of masterpieces of art and architecture. Protestants saw such wealth as proof that the Church placed too much emphasis on worldly things. Lands and riches, they thought, were more appropriate for rulers than religious communities. For this and other reasons, the Church's wealth was an irresistible temptation to many rulers who embraced Protestantism. Between 1536 and 1540, for example, Henry VIII dissolved all 708 of England's monasteries, using their property to help refill his bankrupt royal treasury. As a result, 6,521 monks and 1,560 nuns lost their homes and their way of life, and around 12,000 people who had depended on the monasteries for their jobs or for charity had to look for other means of support.

THE PARISH

For most Renaissance people, Catholic or Protestant, the center of their religious community was their local or parish church. The church was at the heart of village or neighborhood social life in a variety of other ways, too. It functioned as a kind of community center, a place where meetings and other gatherings could take place. City churches often had large open squares or plazas in front of them, where markets were held on different days of the week. In some areas, especially in the country, the churchyard was a favorite location for dances. Churchmen had complained about this for years, and Protestants who followed Calvin were even more upset about it. Calvin himself called dancing "the chief mischief of all mischiefs." Reformers and Catholic priests alike disapproved of the gossiping and flirting that often went on during church services. Many Protestant groups took strong measures to control this behavior, often by making men sit on one side of the church and women on the other.

Inside a Catholic Church

Most Catholic houses of worship were built according to a specific plan. The focal point of the church was the choir, or chancel. This was always in the east of the building. Here was the high altar, where priests conducted Mass and offered Holy Communion. The altar was on a raised platform reached by three steps, which symbolized the Trinity. At the back of the altar there might be an altarpiece, a painting or carved panel showing episodes from the life of Jesus or the saints.

The choir was only for members of the clergy and often was separated from the main part of the church by a screen carved out of wood or stone. While the priests chanted the Mass and other services, the congregation listened from the nave. This was the central section of the church. At the head of the nave, just in front of the choir screen and to the congregation's left, there was a pulpit, a kind of platform raised up high. A priest stood here when he preached a sermon. Most churchgoers had to stand to listen, unless they brought benches or stools from home—there were generally seats only for members of the clergy and for the most prominent people in the congregation.

Catholic churches were decorated as beautifully as their communities could afford, often with precious objects that had been handed down for generations. There might be golden candlesticks, stained-glass windows, ornate wood carvings, and beautiful paintings and statues of Jesus and various saints. On the other hand, in rural villages the church was often a small, plainly decorated building. Sometimes the choir alone had a stone floor, the rest of the building having a floor of packed earth. But there were still beautiful and meaningful objects used in worship, such as the chalice to hold the Communion wine.

Inside a Protestant Church

At the beginning of the Reformation, there were no churches built specifically for Protestant worship. Protestants simply took over the existing church buildings. This was sometimes a violent process, especially in cities, where the Reformation movement was usually stronger than in the countryside. Many Reformers, believing that devotion to saints was un-Christian and kept people from relating directly to God, despised the paintings and statues of saints in Catholic churches. Some Protestants felt that any decoration at all in church distracted worshippers from God's word. There were even those who wanted to rid the churches of organs and other musical instruments, which were thought to be too worldly. On several occasions Protestant mobs fired up by these beliefs stormed churches and monasteries, smashing stained-glass windows, hammering statues to pieces, hacking up wood carvings, and in general destroying every religious image they came upon by any means possible.

The great Christian humanist Erasmus witnessed religious riots in Basel, Switzerland, in 1524 and 1529. He wrote that the rioters were "like men possessed, with anger and rage painted on their faces," and sadly mourned the loss of so much precious and beautiful artwork: "Not a statue was left either in the churches, or the vestibules, or the porches, or the monasteries. The frescoes were obliterated by means of a coating of lime. Whatever would burn was thrown into the fire, and the rest was pounded into fragments. Nothing was spared for love or money."

Aside from their decorations, church buildings had to be adapted in other ways to suit Protestant needs. Catholic worship services did not always include sermons, but Protestant ones did. To stress the importance of sermons and Bible readings, Protestants moved the pulpit into the nave, much closer to the congregation. Calvinists favored a simple wooden pulpit raised only a few steps high. Altars were replaced by communion tables, often set in front of the pulpit. In some churches, the clergy and the congregation's elected elders sat at the communion table to lead the service.

Protestants generally stood up to pray and sat down to listen to the sermon and Bible readings. To emphasize the belief that the clergy and congregation were spiritually equal before God, seating was provided for everyone. In many places, though, noble or wealthy churchgoers still had their

An early Protestant church, known as the Temple of Paradise, in Lyons, France

own family pews, located closest to the front of the church.

Martin Luther did not object to artwork in churches, so long as it expressed proper Lutheran beliefs. Many English churches, especially those far from London—the center of government and the Reform movement—were able to keep much of their Catholic decoration. But Calvinists preferred plain churches and simple worship services. An Italian Calvinist who moved to Geneva was full of praise for the simplicity of religious life in that city: "There are no organs here, no voice of bells, no showy songs, no burning candles or lamps, no relics, pictures, statues, canopies, or splendid robes, no farces or cold ceremonies. The churches are quite free from idolatry."

four

MEN OF GOD

In the Catholic Church, there were two types of clergymen. The secular clergy were parish priests, bishops, cathedral officials, and the like. These men were out in the world (*secula* in Latin), interacting with ordinary people on a day-to-day basis. The regular clergy were those who lived according to a set of guidelines called a rule (*regula* in Latin), mainly monks. Their relationship to the everyday world varied depending on the requirements of their rule.

"IN THE WORLD BUT NOT OF IT"

A priest was empowered to offer Holy Communion, to preach, to bless, and to forgive sins. He could administer all the sacraments except confirmation and holy orders. If he was a parish priest, his main duty was to use these powers to care for the souls of the people of his parish. Someday, through

Catholic clergymen were set apart from their congregations in many ways, including a special haircut called a tonsure.

hard work and good fortune, he might become a bishop. Then he would be able to administer all the sacraments, and would supervise the priests in his diocese. Many Renaissance bishops were also powerful landowners and even territorial rulers—the German city-state of Cologne, for example, was ruled by its bishop.

A man was supposed to be at least twenty-five years old to take holy orders, the sacrament that made him a priest. During much of the Renaissance, however, exceptions were made to this rule for personal or political reasons. For example, Pope Alexander VI made his son Cesare Borgia an archbishop (a very high-ranking priest) at about the age of seventeen.

In theory, many years of study and devotion were necessary to prepare for the priesthood. In reality, this was not always possible. There were many priests who were very learned and devout. But there were also a great number, especially in the countryside, who had little opportunity to learn much Latin (the Church's official language) or to master the Church's teachings. Nevertheless, uneducated country priests were frequently loved and respected by their parishes—they must have had admirable qualities that made up for lack of learning.

Although the secular clergy lived and worked among ordinary people, they were set off from them in important ways. The visible sign of the clergy's dedication to religion was the tonsure, a haircut that left the top of the head bald. Clergymen also had special privileges. They were not required to serve in the military or to pay taxes. If accused of crimes, they could only be tried by the Church's courts.

Since 1074, priests had been forbidden to marry, because all their time and energy were supposed to be devoted to God. The ban on marriage was also another means of marking the unique role of priests, of making them different from other people. A great many priests, though—including high-ranking ones—did live with women and have children. Parishes often accepted this without any problem, even giving a priest's unofficial wife a place of honor at local festivals.

LIVING BY THE RULE

Almost from the beginnings of Christianity, there had been people who wanted to withdraw from the world and turn all their attention to God. Many such people gathered together in small communities devoted to the religious life; these were the first monasteries. Around the year 529, Saint Benedict wrote a book of rules to guide the monks of his Italian monastery. The Rule of Saint Benedict became the basis of monastery life for centuries to come.

All monks vowed themselves, for the rest of their lives, to poverty (they were not allowed to own any personal property), chastity (they could not marry or have relationships with women), and obedience (to the head of the monastery and to the Church's teachings). The rule gave further guidance to their lives. It covered everything from how religious services should be conducted to how much the monks should eat. These guidelines helped the monks to think of God and the monastery community before themselves.

In keeping with their vow of poverty, monks often dressed in simple brown woolen robes. The Rule of Saint Benedict said, "Let the monks not worry about the color or the texture of all these things, but let them be such as can be bought more cheaply."

Falling from Grace

Many monks had extreme difficulty living up to the high standards of behavior demanded by their monastery's rule. A great many monks, of course, remained true to their vows and performed their religious duties faithfully. Even corrupt monks didn't necessarily behave any worse than other European men of the time—but people expected more from monks. Here is the complaint of a German church official, from around 1490:

> *The three vows of religion . . . are as little heeded by these men as if they had never promised to keep them. . . . The whole day is spent in filthy talk; their whole time is given to play and gluttony. . . . In open possession of private property . . . each dwells in his own private lodging. . . . They neither fear nor love God; they have no thought of the life to come, preferring their fleshly lusts to the needs of the soul. . . . They scorn the vow of poverty, know not that of chastity, revile that of obedience. . . . The smoke of their filth ascends all around.*

By the Renaissance, there were a number of different monastic orders. Each had its own rule, altering Saint Benedict's guidelines as needed to reflect the order's specific goals. For example, the Augustinian order (which Martin Luther belonged to) was focused on good works, such as running hospitals, helping the poor, and teaching in schools and universities. The Dominican order's special concerns were to improve people's morals and to make certain that people's beliefs were in line with official Church teachings. Dominicans were often highly educated, with a thorough knowledge of the Church's history, laws, and beliefs, so that they could effectively

preach and teach these beliefs. Some of the Reformation's strongest opponents were members of the Dominican order.

New orders were established in the wake of the Reformation, as the Catholic Church took various measures to reform itself from within. The most influential of these new groups was the Society of Jesus, or Jesuits. Members of this order, founded in 1540 by Ignatius Loyola, took the three traditional monks' vows and added a fourth: to serve the pope without hesitation, doing whatever he commanded for the sake of spreading the faith. The Society of Jesus focused its efforts on missionary work and education. In its first twenty-five years alone, the Society established 100 colleges and 130 monasteries. Jesuit teaching and preaching swayed Poland, most of Hungary, and parts of Germany away from Protestantism and back to Catholicism. The Society sent numerous missionaries to non-European countries, including India and Japan. Along with members of the Franciscan order, Jesuits also played a major role as missionaries in Spain's New World colonies.

From Soldier to Saint

Ignatius Loyola, the founder of the Society of Jesus, was born into a noble family in northern Spain in 1491. As a boy he received little education, but he did love to read, especially popular tales of knights, love, and adventure. He grew up to become a soldier. When he was thirty years old, he was severely wounded in battle. At home in his family's castle, he had a long recovery and couldn't do much except read. The only two books in the castle were a life of Jesus and a collection of stories about the saints. At first Loyola was bored with these. But as he reread them, he became impressed with the heroic things the saints did for the sake of their faith. He vowed that once he recovered, he would spend the rest of his life as a soldier for Jesus and Mary.

At first Loyola thought he would go to Jerusalem and fight to take the Holy City from its Turkish Muslim rulers. On his way to the port of Barcelona, where he hoped to get a ship for the East, he realized that the saints he admired fought with no weapon but their faith. Stopping at a Benedictine monastery, he left his sword at an altar dedicated to Mary, made vows of poverty and chastity, and received Communion. He then lived in a cave for ten months. He spent this time praying, doing penance for his past sins, and meditating on the life of Jesus. Sometimes he had visions of Jesus, Mary, and the Trinity. His meditations and visions led to the composition of his influential book *The Spiritual Exercises*, which continues to inspire Catholics throughout the world today.

After his months of prayer and meditation in the cave, Loyola resumed his journey to Jerusalem. He reached the Holy City in the summer of 1523, intending to convert the Muslims to Christianity. For the sake of keeping the peace, he was persuaded to give up this idea and return to Spain. At the age of thirty-three, he decided to go back to grammar school so that he could learn Latin. He then went to college in Paris, to study for the priesthood. In 1534 he, his two roommates, and seven other men formed the Company of Jesus. They set off on foot for Venice, where they hoped to get a ship for the Holy Land. This proved impossible, for Venice was at war with the Turks. Loyola and his followers decided instead to go to Rome and offer themselves to serve the pope. In 1540 Pope Paul III gave his approval to Loyola to found the Society of Jesus. Loyola worked tirelessly for the Society until his death in 1556. In 1622 the Church declared him a saint.

Saint Ignatius Loyola receiving a vision during Mass, painted by Peter Paul Rubens

PROTESTANT MINISTERS

One of Martin Luther's most important ideas was "the priesthood of all believers." According to this, no one needed a priest or anyone else to help them communicate with God—each person could and should pray and confess to God directly. Most Protestant churches did away with priests. Instead they had clergymen who were generally called ministers or pastors. *Minister* is from the Latin word that means "to serve," for these men were regarded as servants of God. *Pastor* comes from the Latin for "shepherd." Like a shepherd guarding sheep, a church's pastor was supposed to guide and protect his congregation.

Clergymen in the Church of England continued to be called priests, but they were not set apart from the rest of society like Catholic priests were. The most obvious sign of this was that priests in the Church of England, like all other Protestant clergymen, were both allowed and encouraged to get married.

One of a Protestant minister's most important jobs was to preach sermons. In his sermons, the minister was supposed to help the congregation understand the Bible and how it applied to their own lives. To be a good preacher, the minister had to have a thorough understanding of scripture and excellent writing and public-speaking skills. This required a particular kind of education. In many areas that embraced Protestantism, new schools to educate ministers quickly sprang up. For example, as soon as the leaders of Nuremberg, Germany, decided to make their city-state Lutheran, in 1525, they set up a school to train ministers. They brought in Philipp Melanchthon, one of Luther's closest associates, to plan the course of study.

Education was, in fact, one of the Reformation's greatest gifts to Europe. Most Reformers taught that everyone should be able to read the Bible for themselves. For this reason, Protestant communities generally did their utmost to make sure that every man, woman, and child learned to read.

Five

WOMEN AND THE CHURCH

In Renaissance Europe there were many negative opinions about women. Although peasant women worked in the fields alongside men, and city women worked at almost every trade that men did, women were still thought of as weaker and less intelligent than men. Most authorities believed that women had to have the protection and guidance of men, and many laws reflected this. The inferiority of women was one subject on which most Catholics and Protestants agreed.

BRIDES OF CHRIST

In the early years of Christianity, women played an active part in spreading and supporting the new faith. The Catholic Church continued to give women roles in religion. Women could not join the secular clergy, but they

Two views of a Catholic lady holding a rosary, a string of beads used to help with concentration during prayers. The main prayer said with the rosary was addressed to Mary, the model of Christian womanhood.

could join monasteries and become nuns. As nuns, they made the same life-long vows of poverty, chastity, and obedience that monks did. A nun's vows were sealed by a ring that she wore to show that she had turned away from marriage and the world and was wedded to Christ.

Even so, nuns faced many of the same prejudices and restrictions as other women. The Church taught that women were naturally more sinful than men, and that women distracted men from religion. Women were forbidden to preach, to serve as priests, or even to assist priests during religious services. Women's monasteries were almost always supervised by men—the head of a men's monastery of the same order, or the bishop of the local diocese. Most importantly, every house of nuns had at least one male chaplain. This priest (or group of priests) conducted Mass for the nuns, heard their confessions, blessed them, and received new nuns' vows. No woman was permitted to do any of these things.

Most women's monastic rules required the nuns to stay in the convent at all times, although some Renaissance convents had become fairly relaxed about this requirement. Many women thrived in the seclusion and discipline of a monastery, which offered them the opportunity to devote themselves to prayer and study. A monastery was often the only place where an intelligent woman was allowed to pursue an education, to write books, or to teach others.

Nuns often wrote of their happiness that they would not have to marry someone they might not love (most Renaissance marriages, especially in the upper classes, were arranged by the parents). They were also safe from the dangers of childbirth, which killed a great many women during this period. Renaissance nuns rarely did any kind of physical work. They were almost always from the upper classes; women from lower-class families also lived in convents, though not as full nuns, and did the cooking, cleaning, and so on. Prayer was the main occupation of both monks and nuns, who generally took part in eight or nine religious services a day. Some monastic orders offered women other kinds of fulfilling work, such as teaching the

An Unwilling Nun

The Renaissance saw an increase in complaints about nuns not living up to their vows and the simplicity of the monastic rules. There were indeed convents where nuns lived in luxury, ate gourmet meals, entertained visitors, spent their time playing the lute or doing elegant embroidery instead of praying, and left the monastery walls for picnics and other social outings. Part of the reason for such behavior was that a great many women were sent into convents against their will. Some were only nine years old, or even younger, when they began monastic life.

Parents placed girls in convents for various reasons, but the most common one was economic. Although a nun's family had to make a gift of money or property to the monastery she joined, this gift was much smaller than the dowry owed to her husband if she married. Many upper-class families, especially in Italy, were not willing or able to provide dowries for all their daughters. This was particularly true of parents who were trying to make sure their sons would have large inheritances. So, to save money, one or more daughters might be sent away to become nuns, often whether they wanted to or not. To such women, the convent was a prison.

Arcangela Tarabotti of Venice was placed in a monastery as a child and became a nun at the age of sixteen. She felt no calling to the religious life and hated it, but had no choice in the matter. Her anger was expressed in a book she wrote, *Simplicity Betrayed*, which was published two years after her death in 1652. Although Tarabotti lived slightly after the Renaissance, her words give voice to all the unwilling nuns of the earlier period:

> It seems to me, when I see one of these unfortunate girls so betrayed by
> their own fathers, that I see that which happens to the little song bird,

which in its pure simplicity, there between the leaves of the trees or along the banks of rivers, goes with sweet murmur and with gentle harmony . . . when there comes a sly net and it is caught and deprived of its dear liberty. In the same way these unhappy girls, born under an unfortunate star, pass the years of their innocent girlhood, and . . . please the ear and delight the soul of the base fathers who, deceitful, . . . think of nothing but to remove them from sight as soon as possible and so bury them alive in cloisters for the whole of their lives, bound with indissoluble knots.

Four German nuns praying during a church service

young—many convents included boarding schools for girls. A woman who truly felt a religious calling, in a community of like-minded women, could often find more support, more dignity, and more opportunities for self-expression in a monastery than anywhere else in Renaissance Europe.

Nuns and the Reformation

To sincere, dedicated nuns in many countries, the Reformation was a horrible blow. Most Protestant governments eventually closed down all monasteries, often turning monks and nuns out into the streets. This was especially hard on the nuns. As women, they had little freedom outside the convent and might have no way to earn a living. They generally had to marry or return to their parents' homes.

Many nuns fought the closing of their monasteries. Most were not successful, but a few were. Caritas Pirckheimer was head of a convent of about sixty women in Nuremberg, Germany. From one of the city's most influential families, she was highly educated and had contacts with notable scholars all over northern Europe. In her memoirs she described the struggle to save her monastery. For instance, one day three women, supported by a mob, came to take their daughters away from the convent: "The wives then bade the children come out with kind words, saying that if they did not do so willingly, they would pull them out forcibly. . . . The children cried that they did not want to leave the pious, holy convent."

The girls' protests did not win out—their families ended up taking them home by force. But Caritas Pirckheimer did not give up her fight to keep the convent open. The Nuremberg city council finally agreed. The monastery was forbidden to receive any new members, but all the nuns were allowed to remain in the religious life that they loved until their deaths.

SERVING GOD IN THE HOME

As they studied the Bible, Reformers noted that some of Jesus' disciples were married and that all the holy men of the Old Testament had wives and children. This helped convince Protestants that God regarded marriage as the ideal state for human beings. The Catholic Church had always taught that taking holy orders or monastic vows was the most righteous way of life. Now Reformers argued that rejecting marriage and making a vow of chastity was against the will of God. Luther himself, to set the example, married an ex-nun, Katherine von Bora, in 1525, and had six children with her. The

An English lady with her two sons. Like many mothers, both Catholic and Protestant, she has probably been her children's first teacher, helping them learn reading, writing, and basic prayers and religious beliefs.

Two Women of Spirit

Two of the most dynamic religious women of the sixteenth century were Angela Merici and Teresa of Avila. Both founded important new religious societies, within which they treated rich women and poor women as equals. Both were later declared saints. But each had a distinct vision of how a Catholic woman could best serve God. While Angela Merici wanted religious women to be active in the world, Teresa of Avila believed that nuns (and monks) could live more holy lives if they were completely cut off from the world.

Like a number of women since the thirteenth century, for many years Angela Merici followed a modified version of Saint Francis of Assisi's monastic rule while living in her own home. When she was in her fifties, she felt called to organize a group of young women who would be dedicated to prayer and charity. Merici's goal was for these women to actively serve people as Jesus' apostles had done. In 1535 she established the Company of Saint Ursula in Brescia, Italy.

The Ursulines, as they were called, made a lifelong vow of chastity as a loving sacrifice to God. During Merici's lifetime, they usually lived in their family homes. The Company helped members without families find jobs as live-in housekeepers or governesses in respectable homes. The Ursulines met together twice a month. The younger members were called daughters and received guidance from the mothers, older married women or widows. The mothers directed the group's activities, which included nursing, assisting the poor, instructing people in basic Catholic beliefs, and teaching in schools, especially girls' schools.

Ursuline communities were set up in France as well as in many parts of Italy. Church authorities, however, were always a little nervous about the Company's independence. After Angela Merici died in 1540, the Church pressured most of the Ursulines to live in convents and become a traditional monastic order. Only in Brescia and nearby Milan were they permitted to go on working in the world. Yet inside or outside the convent, the Ursulines continued to play an active and important role as educators.

When Teresa of Avila entered the religious life, she belonged to a convent in which the nuns were allowed to wear jewelry and had finely furnished suites of rooms. They were even permitted to leave to visit relatives. In the 1540s she began to receive visions of Jesus. As she later wrote, "I saw Him with the eyes of the soul more clearly than I could ever have seen Him with those of the body." Around 1560 she had an especially powerful religious experience. In a vision, an angel came to her: "In his hands I saw a long golden spear and at the end of the iron tip I seemed to see a point of fire. With this he seemed to pierce my heart several times. . . . When he drew it out . . . he left me completely afire with a great love of God."

Teresa came to feel that her visions were guiding her to leave her convent for a stricter life of poverty and prayer. In 1562 she founded her own monastery and a new order, the Discalced Carmelites. (*Discalced* means "shoeless"; the nuns wore rope sandals as a sign of humility.) Teresa's nuns had no furniture and were allowed no guests. They were so closed off from the world that they even covered their windows with cloth to block off any view of the outside. They supported themselves by spinning and sewing, leaving their finished work on a revolving disk built into the convent wall. Anyone from the outside could take what they wanted from the outer half of the disk and leave food or other donations in exchange. Teresa and her nuns soon became well known for their holiness. Within a few years Teresa was asked to help establish similar monasteries throughout Spain, not only for nuns but also for monks. Teresa worked tirelessly on this mission, overcoming many difficulties, until her death in 1582.

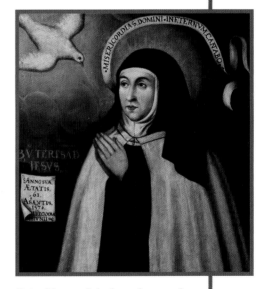

Saint Teresa of Avila at the age of sixty-one, with a dove representing the Holy Spirit. The Latin words above her head mean, "I will praise the Lord's mercy in song forever."

marriage was such a happy one that Luther once declared, "The greatest gift of God to man is a pious, kindly, God-fearing, home-loving wife." The Reformers, however, were still convinced that women were weaker and less intelligent than men. Their weakness, though, was made up for by their ability to bear children. In fact, the Reformers thought, giving birth was one of the noblest works that women could do for God.

All Protestant women were expected to marry, have children, help their husbands, and run a home. The Reformers considered this the ideal Christian life for a woman. As Luther wrote, "If a mother of a family wishes to please and serve God, let her not do what the papists [Catholics] are accustomed to doing: running to churches, fasting, counting prayers, etc. But let her care for the family, let her educate and teach her children, let her do her task in the kitchen. If she does these things in faith in the Son of God, and hopes that she pleases God on account of Christ, she is holy and blessed."

Protestant guidelines for marriage were based on the Bible. In the New Testament, husbands were instructed to love their wives, but wives were told to obey their husbands: "Wives, be subject to your husbands, as to the Lord. For the husband is the head of the wife as Christ is the head of the church. . . . As the church is subject to Christ, so let wives also be subject in everything to their husbands" (Ephesians 5: 22–24). While Catholic women relied on their priests for spiritual guidance, in Protestantism the husband, as head of the family, was in charge of his wife's spiritual life. He was expected to teach her and to keep her from sinning. He was also supposed to take care of her just as he cared for himself. In return, the wife should always be ready to help him in every area of life.

For many Protestant husbands and wives, their shared faith brought them close. They prayed and studied the Bible at home together, often with their children. A minister's wife might be able to participate in, or at least listen to, religious discussions between her husband and his students or friends. Protestant women also did charitable work for their congregations and communities. Many women thrived in this atmosphere and played their own role in spreading the Reform movement.

A Letter from a Minister's Wife

Katherine Zell's husband, Matthias, was a former priest. He became a Protestant pastor in Strasbourg, a German city within the Holy Roman Empire.* When Catholic authorities criticized Matthias for marrying, Katherine spoke out in a well-argued essay defending the right of ministers to marry. Being a pastor's wife allowed Katherine Zell to live a life that she found very fulfilling, as she wrote in a letter to the citizens of Strasbourg near the end of her life:

> *That I learned to understand and helped to acknowledge the Gospel I shall let God declare. That I married my pious husband and for this endured slander and lies, God knows. The work which I carried on both in the house and out is known both by those who already rest in God and those who are still living, how I helped to establish the Gospel, took in the exiled, comforted the homeless refugees, furthered the church, preaching and the schools, God will remember even if the world may forget or did not notice. . . . I honored, cherished, and sheltered many great, learned men, with care, work, and expense. . . . I listened to their conversation and their preaching, I read their books and their letters and they were glad to receive mine . . . and I must express how fond I was of all the old, great learned men and founders of the Church of Christ, how much I enjoyed listening to their talk of holy things and how my heart was joyful in these things.*

*Today Strasbourg is part of France, very close to the border with Germany.

Like men, women participated in the prayers and hymn singing in Protestant churches. However, they could not preach or take any kind of leadership role, for the Bible said, "The women should keep silent in the churches. For they are not permitted to speak, but should be subordinate, as even the law says. If there is anything they desire to know, let them ask their husbands at home. For it is shameful for a woman to speak in church" (1 Corinthians 14:34–35). Women might sometimes give religious instruction to other women, though, and mothers were expected to help their children to be good Christians. In special circumstances (and outside of church), women might also preach to other women. For example, a group of Protestant women went to a Geneva convent several times to try to persuade the nuns to leave it (with little success).

WOMEN UNDER SUSPICION: THE WITCH HUNTS

Both Catholic and Protestant churches believed that women needed male guidance and supervision. The different branches of Renaissance Christianity generally agreed on something else: the existence of evil witches. Until the thirteenth century, the Church had taught that belief in witchcraft was an illusion caused by the devil. Gradually, though, influential churchmen accepted and spread the idea that there were witches who flew through the air to gatherings in the night, where they rejected Jesus and promised to serve the devil. They were said to cause storms, damage crops, harm livestock, ruin wine, kill babies, and the like.

After the invention of the printing press, books and pamphlets describing these witches were published, and a great many copies were sold. Fear of witchcraft grew, and governments set up procedures for putting suspected witches on trial. The accused were almost always tortured until they confessed. Condemned witches were executed, and their bodies were often burned at the stake—the usual punishment for heresy, a crime against religion.

Women with mental illness were in great danger of being accused as witches. In other cases, mental illness might be interpreted as demonic possession, and priests could be summoned to exorcise, or cast out, the demon, as in this scene.

From about the last part of the fifteenth century to the middle of the seventeenth century, thousands of witch hunts were carried on by government or religious officials. They were most common in the Holy Roman Empire, peaking in the 1500s and early 1600s. In all, around 110,000 Europeans were accused of witchcraft. About 60,000 of them were executed. (These numbers are low estimates—some sources give numbers as high as 1,500,000.)

An average of about 75 percent of the people accused of witchcraft were women—but in some areas, it was as high as 95 percent. We know of one German town where witch hunters accused all but two of the townswomen of witchcraft. Most commonly, throughout Europe, suspected witches were poor, uneducated women over the age of forty. They were often sharp-tongued or quarrelsome—or perhaps just too "uppity" for their neighbors. Midwives, who delivered babies and treated women's health problems, were frequently accused. So were other women healers—sometimes even when their cures worked. But when a witch hunt was under way, no woman was free from suspicion.

Six

HOLY DAYS AND EVERY DAY

R eligion was woven into the lives of Renaissance Europeans in a variety of ways. It influenced the holidays they celebrated, the names they gave their children, the clothes they wore, the food they ate, the way they handled birth and death. Even people who did not have strong personal religious beliefs could not help being affected by the Catholicism or Protestantism of the time.

HOLY DAYS

During the Renaissance, all holidays had a religious significance. In Catholic areas, there were many holidays throughout the year. For example, the Italian city of Florence celebrated around forty feast days; Venice celebrated around ninety. These holy days included Christmas, Easter, and other days that honored events in the life of Jesus. There were also many

Singing was an important and much loved part of many church services, especially on holy days. This choir seems to be particularly enthusiastic.

holidays that commemorated the life of his mother, Mary. The other celebrations were devoted to various saints.

For all of these holy days, people got a full or half day off from work. The celebrations often included elaborate processions, or parades, in which beautiful statues of saints were carried through the streets. On some holidays there were plays in which Bible stories were acted out. Church services might include special music and prayers. Holidays were also times for dances, feasts, bonfires, fireworks, races, and performances by jugglers, magicians, and acrobats.

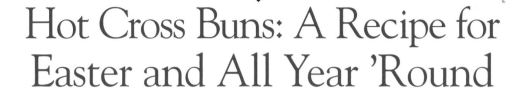

Hot Cross Buns: A Recipe for Easter and All Year 'Round

An Easter tradition in Renaissance England was baking hot cross buns. The cross of icing on top of each bun symbolized Jesus' death and resurrection. A variety of folk beliefs surrounded the buns, too. People kept Easter's hot cross buns long after the holiday was over, for it was said that they would never go moldy. Many people believed that the buns brought good luck and that they could cure diseases in people and in livestock. Sailors even carried hot cross buns with them on voyages as a protection against shipwrecks.

Whether you celebrate Easter or not, you can still experience a bit of Renaissance culture and enjoy delicious hot cross buns. To make them, you will need a bread or roll mix, such as Pillsbury's Hot Roll Mix, and any additional ingredients required for the mix, along with:

1/4 cup sugar
1/4 teaspoon cinnamon
1/8 teaspoon nutmeg
1/4 cup raisins

1/2 cup sifted confectioners' sugar
2 teaspoons hot milk
1/4 teaspoon vanilla extract

Mix the sugar, cinnamon, nutmeg, and raisins together. Add this mixture to the flour in the roll mix. Follow the directions on the roll mix box to make the dough for the buns. After the dough has risen the first time, shape it into 18 balls and arrange them on a greased cookie sheet. Cover the sheet with a clean dish towel and let the buns rise to about twice their original size. While they are rising, preheat your oven to 425°F. Bake the buns until they are golden brown (about 20 minutes).

When the buns are cool, combine the confectioners' sugar, hot milk, and vanilla extract. Mix until smooth. Drizzle this glaze from a spoon to make an equal-armed cross on top of each bun. Let the glaze harden, then eat and enjoy!

Many Protestants objected to the nonreligious activities that took place on holy days. They also objected to certain of the holidays themselves. Most Protestants put much less importance on Mary than Catholics did, and almost no importance at all on other saints. Protestant communities therefore celebrated far fewer holidays. In England, for example, the number of recognized festivals was reduced from ninety-five before the Reformation to twenty-seven afterward. A number of Protestant groups celebrated only Christmas and Easter. Some of the strictest followers of Jean Calvin recognized Easter alone.

In cities with both Protestants and Catholics, holidays were sometimes a source of conflict. Protestants complained about Catholics not working on holidays. Catholics were insulted that Protestants did work. In some cities, Lutheran or Calvinist women would sit right by their windows to sew and spin so that Catholics passing by in religious processions would have to notice them. In one French city, on a couple of occasions, some Protestant women did their laundry on Catholic holidays, and Catholics threw the clothes into the river.

The Lord's Day

Both Catholics and Protestants celebrated Sunday as a holiday and a day off from work. In many places, such as England, the law required people to attend church every week and to take Communion a certain number of times a year. (And from 1570 into the 1590s, the law also demanded that Englishmen, except for nobles, wear woolen caps to church—part of a government plan to support the nation's wool industry.) After the worship service, or between morning and evening services, there was often time for fun and relaxation.

During the reign of Queen Elizabeth I, English country people enjoyed playing a rough form of football on Sunday afternoons. This kind of thing was fiercely criticized by Puritan writers and preachers: "Any exercise which withdraweth us from godliness, either upon the sabbath or any other day, is wicked and to be forbidden. . . . As concerning football-playing, I protest unto you it may rather be called a friendly kind of fight than a play or recreation, a bloody and murdering practice than a fellowly sport or pastime."

Puritans and other followers of Calvin took very seriously the biblical commandment "Remember the sabbath day, to keep it holy" (Exodus 20:8). Sunday was a day of rest from regular work, but it was also the Lord's day. Puritan church services could be very long, with sermons lasting two or three hours. People were expected to spend most of the rest of the day in Bible study and similar activities—definitely not playing football.

DAILY FAITH

Some Reformers were especially concerned with making sure that religion guided every part of people's lives. Jean Calvin thought that government and society should be run according to the Bible. He put this belief into action when the independent city of Geneva, Switzerland, invited him to head the Reformed Church there in 1541. Under his influence, the city council passed laws that regulated almost every aspect of people's behavior. People could be punished for not going to church, for arriving late to church, and for not taking Communion often enough. Dancing, card playing, gambling, swearing, and singing irreligious songs were against the law. Women could be put in jail for wearing makeup, elaborate hairstyles, or immodest clothing. Parents were required to give their children biblical names and could not use the names of Catholic saints. Books that disagreed with Reformed teachings were banned. Only religious plays could be performed; eventually even these were outlawed.

Both Catholic and Protestant authorities wanted religion to be a part

Jean Calvin in his study. Calvin was extremely learned and wrote commentaries on almost every book of the Bible.

of everyday life, and for a great many people it was. Even the passage of time (in the days before the wristwatch) was marked by the church. In many towns and villages, both Catholic and Protestant, the day began with church bells ringing to wake people up. In the English countryside, the highest-pitched bell was rung to let harvesters know when it was time to go out to the fields, and again when it was time to leave off work in the evening. In Catholic churches the bells rang at intervals throughout the day to signal the time for various prayers.

Catholics had standard prayers that were recited in Latin, both in and out of church. The most important were the *Pater Noster* ("Our Father," also known as the Lord's Prayer) and the *Ave Maria* ("Hail Mary"). The *Pater Noster* was a prayer that Jesus had taught to his disciples. The *Ave Maria* was based on the words that the angel Gabriel spoke to Mary when he told her that she would be the mother of Jesus. Protestants also used the Lord's Prayer—except it was prayed in the everyday language of the people. Luther translated the prayer into German early on, and other Reformers followed his lead.

A Farmer's Devotion

A churchman during the Renaissance left this description of an Italian villager, offering him as an example of a humble man living a devout Christian life:

> *When he is not tending the herds and is at home in winter or when it rains, or during such times, he always goes to Mass; he always makes the sign of the cross when the Ave Maria [bell] tolls, he recites the Ave Maria, crossing himself first, he rests the oxen from their work at that time, blesses the bread and offers thanks to God after he has eaten; when he goes out to Mass he has a rosary in his hands; in church he is respectful and recites the rosary, and so he performs all the duties of a good Christian.*

THROUGH THE STAGES OF LIFE

One of the beliefs that Catholics and Protestants shared was the importance of baptism. In this ceremony, a priest or minister welcomed a child into the Christian community by sprinkling it with water (or sometimes briefly dunking it into water) in memory of Jesus' baptism. Because babies during this time period often did not live for very long, baptism was usually performed shortly after birth. Otherwise, according to many people, the soul of an unbaptized child who died would go to hell. One group of Protestants, however, did not baptize infants or children. Known as Anabaptists, they believed that people should not be baptized until they were adults and could willingly embrace the Christian faith.

Marriage was one of the stages of life that both Catholics and Protestants celebrated in church. In this Catholic wedding ceremony, the priest is blessing the bride and groom's union.

Childhood experiences varied according to a number of factors. Most Renaissance children received little education because they had to help their parents work. A Catholic child from a well-off family might be sent to school in a monastery. Public schools were beginning to appear in greater number, especially in cities. However, most of them charged fees that few families could afford. Calvin's Geneva looked to the future by requiring that all children go to school. Well-to-do parents were expected to contribute to the costs of running the schools, but poor children could attend for free. The students, both girls and boys, learned reading, writing, arithmetic, and religion. For many years, though, there was no public secondary school for girls to attend—usually, only boys were able to continue their formal education.

Many boys, and a small number of girls, became apprentices to learn a craft or trade. In this area, too, religion could play a role. In Catholic communities, each craft and trade had its own patron saint. The craftspeople would celebrate this saint's feast day and might attend a church dedicated to the saint. As the Reformation took hold, it became common for apprentices to have to meet religious requirements. For example, in Nuremburg after 1525, only Lutherans were allowed to become apprentices.

As we have seen, Catholic and Protestant ideas about marriage were the same in some ways and different in others. Two things that almost everyone agreed on was that engagements should be publicly announced and that wedding ceremonies should be held in church. This had not always been the case in the past. The sixteenth century also saw an increasing emphasis on the bride and groom promising to love and care for each other. The Church of England's *Book of Common Prayer* put this promise into words that are still heard at numerous weddings today: "I . . . take thee . . . to have and to hold from this day forward, for better, for worse, for richer, for poorer, in sickness and in health, to love and to cherish, till death us depart [divide], according to God's holy ordinance: and thereto I plight thee my troth."

Seven

LEARNING TOLERANCE

In 1555, the Holy Roman Emperor signed a treaty that granted German princes and dukes the right to decide whether their territories would be Catholic or Lutheran. Almost everywhere, in fact, it was European rulers who ultimately decided what people's religion would be. Separation between church and state was almost completely unknown. If a ruler became Protestant, he made Protestantism the state religion. Every Christian in the country was generally expected to follow the same religious path.

MARTYRS ON BOTH SIDES

Whether in a Catholic or Protestant country, anyone in a religious minority could have a difficult time. Part of this was a result of the government's involvement with religion. Most rulers and independent city governments believed that a population that was split between different churches could not be effectively governed. The general opinion was that religious unity was necessary for national strength.

Many Protestant countries regarded the pope as a foreign power. Catholics were therefore easily suspected of treason because of their acceptance of the pope's authority. The suspicion was strengthened when Catholic subjects did, sometimes, plot rebellions against Protestant rulers, as in England during the reign of Queen Elizabeth.

England between Two Religions

In most of Europe, once a ruler decided to either remain Catholic or switch to Protestantism, the country's official religion did not change afterward. England, however, was a different case. When Henry VIII established the Church of England in 1534, he accepted nearly all Catholic beliefs except the authority of the pope. (He did, however, close all of England's monasteries and take over their property and income.) During his reign, Protestants who rejected other important Catholic teachings were punished as heretics—people who rejected and endangered religious truth—and treated as harshly as Catholics who remained loyal to the pope. Henry's son, Edward VI, on the other hand, was a much more dedicated Protestant. During his short reign (1547–1553) English replaced Latin as the language for worship services, images of saints were destroyed or removed from churches, and priests were allowed to marry. Many Catholics were put in prison, and two were executed for heresy.

When Edward's half sister Mary Tudor took the throne, the nation's religion changed once again, for Mary was an ardent Catholic. When she first became queen, she declared that she would not force her subjects to follow religious beliefs that were against their conscience. Instead, she hoped that Protestants could be convinced to convert to Catholicism by

Sir Thomas More, England's great humanist writer, was one of many Renaissance people who were killed because of their religious beliefs. The Catholic Church declared More a saint in 1935.

peaceful and reasonable means. In 1555, however, Mary began to allow the persecution of Protestants, and soon she encouraged it. Three hundred or so Protestants were executed during her reign. These martyrdoms strengthened the faith and determination of Protestants, and made many Catholics ashamed of the violence that was done in the name of their church.

In 1558 Mary died and her half sister Elizabeth, a Protestant, became England's ruler. One of her first actions as queen was to forge a compromise between Protestantism and Catholicism. She again made English the language of worship, authorized the publication of an English Bible, and permitted priests to marry. At the same time, she kept some of the Catholic Church's ceremonies, required priests to wear special robes (like Catholic priests, but unlike ministers in many Protestant groups), and supported traditional-style church music. All English citizens had to attend Church of England services, but there was tolerance for people's private religious beliefs.

Most of the people were happy with Elizabeth's compromise, but the country's religious problems still weren't over. In 1570 the pope excommunicated Elizabeth and gave Catholic rulers of other countries permission to overthrow her. In the early 1580s a group of Catholic nobles plotted against Elizabeth, and the Spanish ambassador was involved in a conspiracy to depose her. These and similar events made Elizabeth's government so suspicious of Catholics that in 1585 all Catholic priests were banished from England.

Then Spain declared war, with the pope's blessing, and partly for the purpose of making England a Catholic country again. Jesuit missionaries who had come to England to try to convert people to Catholicism were regarded as spies for the pope or for Spain. They were treated severely whenever they were caught. One Jesuit described the scene in England following the defeat of the Spanish Armada in 1588, after fears of a Spanish invasion were quelled: "The Spanish Fleet had exasperated the people against the Catholics. . . . Everywhere a hunt was being organized for Catholics and their houses searched." Even Elizabeth, one of Europe's most able rulers, could not fully overcome the religious intolerance of her age.

The problem was that both sides were sure that they were absolutely right—their form of Christianity was the only true faith. Anything that differed was seen as a threat, and anyone on the "wrong" side was doomed to eternal suffering in hell. Catholics branded Protestants as heretics, and Protestants did the same to Catholics. In addition, mainstream Protestants joined with Catholics in condemning Anabaptists and other "radical" Protestant sects. The Catholic Church and many Protestant authorities agreed that heretics were enemies of God and deserved the worst possible punishment. This punishment was frequently public execution by burning.

Inquisitions

Since the 1200s the Church had had a special court to find, try, and punish heretics. It was called the Inquisition. By the 1400s it was not very active, except in Spain. There, the Spanish Inquisition pursued not only Christian heretics but also converts to Christianity who were suspected of returning to their original Muslim or Jewish practices. From 1483 to 1498 alone, the Spanish Inquisition executed more than two thousand people. After the Reformation, it persecuted Protestants as well. The Spanish Inquisition also operated in regions ruled by Spain, especially the Low Countries (modern Belgium, Luxembourg, and the Netherlands). Antwerp was the first Low Countries city to have Protestant martyrs when two monks who had accepted Luther's teachings were burned at the stake in 1523. By 1546, roughly one thousand Anabaptists had been executed in the Low Countries.

In 1542 the Catholic Church reorganized the Inquisition to combat Protestantism in Italy. Before long there were few Protestants left on the peninsula—most of those who had not been arrested had fled for their lives, settling in Switzerland or Germany. In 1549 King Henry II of France set up his own commission to hunt down and prosecute heretics. Sixty Protestants were burned within three years. As in other inquisitions at this

Both Catholic and Protestant leaders tried to control the ideas that their people could read about. Both sides burned books that were thought to threaten the religious or political order.

time, anyone who owned books or pamphlets written by Luther or other Reformers was suspect. It was illegal to print, sell, or possess these written materials, and they were destroyed when they were found. The burning of banned books was a common practice among both Catholics and Protestants.

In places where Reformers gained government control, they could be almost as ruthless as the Inquisition. Sir Thomas More, the great writer and statesman, was beheaded in 1535 for rejecting Henry VIII's authority over the church in England. Many of Luther's followers urged German governments to give the death penalty to people who practiced "false religion." Geneva burned its first heretic in 1553. In the 1570s Calvinists temporarily gained control of many places in the Low Countries. Their violence against Catholics prompted a poet in Amsterdam to write, "They who at first asked for no more than to live in freedom, / Now have their liberty, but will not give it to others."

LOOKING FORWARD

The sixteenth century's various forms of Christianity gave many people the spiritual guidance and certainty that they longed for. But the religious conflict also created widespread suffering. From 1546 to 1555, Holy Roman Emperor Charles V and the Catholic rulers of German territories warred against German Protestant rulers. In 1560 France entered into thirty-eight years of civil war, with Catholics and Protestants fighting one another all over the country. The worst episode during these Wars of Religion was the Saint Bartholomew's Day Massacre, which began on August 24, 1572. Catholic mobs attacked and killed Protestants, known as Huguenots, in the streets of Paris. The violence spread to the countryside and to other cities and lasted almost a week. Thousands of Huguenots died. In 1598 the battles and riots finally died down when the Edict of Nantes granted religious freedom to Protestants.

Like many people witnessing the events of the French Wars of Religion, Michel de Montaigne was filled with dismay by the violence around him. He saw that the wars were "the true school of . . . inhumanity." Montaigne, a retired civil servant from a noble family, found comfort in the activity of writing. He invented a new literary form, the personal essay, which he used for self-examination. He felt that "all the evils of this world are engendered by those who teach us not to be aware of our own ignorance." Through self-awareness, according to Montaigne, a person would increase in tolerance and good sense, and would not give way to extreme behaviors. In other words, once you realize that you don't know everything, you are much less likely to be judgmental or cruel to others.

A Third Way

Some years before Montaigne, the great scholar Erasmus had also written in favor of tolerance. Erasmus was able to see both sides of the debate between Protestants and Catholics. He personally preferred a simple form of Christianity, yet he remained loyal to the Catholic Church. He could not join Luther in rejecting the Church's teachings about the importance of good works and of human beings having free will to choose good or evil. Erasmus nevertheless hoped that the Church could be purified of corruption and thought that it shouldn't be necessary to choose between Catholicism and Protestantism. He believed there was a third way, a way of communication instead of conflict. The Catholic Church, he said, could be reformed gradually, from the inside.

For Erasmus and his followers, the key to reforming both church and society was knowledge. The better educated people were, the better they would be able to recognize and understand religious truth. Truth, Erasmus believed, would always win out in any reasonable discussion among knowledgeable people. It made much more sense, meanwhile, to accept differences

One of Erasmus's most famous works, The Praise of Folly, *poked fun at many human failings. Yet, though Erasmus never ignored these shortcomings, he remained convinced that if people had access to knowledge, they would always choose to do good.*

of opinion on religion than to use violence or other extreme measures to try to force everyone to agree to the same set of beliefs.

Throughout the sixteenth century, Erasmus and Montaigne were joined by a few other voices speaking for tolerance and true religious freedom. Among these voices were some of the Anabaptists. Because of the persecution they endured from government-supported churches on both sides, Anabaptists became strong advocates of separating church and state. During the 1600s, this idea would be taken up by more and more people, including the founders of the American colonies of Rhode Island and Pennsylvania. In the 1700s, separation of church and state was championed by the likes of Thomas Jefferson and James Madison.

The success of the American Revolution brought about a true revolution in society and government's attitude toward matters of faith. As the new United States took shape, James Madison spearheaded the creation of the Bill of Rights, ten amendments to the Constitution that would guarantee Americans' personal liberty. The very first statement in the First Amendment is, "Congress shall make no law respecting an establishment of religion, or prohibiting the free exercise thereof." This affirmation of people's most basic right, to decide for themselves how to relate (or not relate) to the divine, at last held out the promise of real religious freedom. The struggles of the sixteenth century remind us how precious this freedom truly is.

GLOSSARY

alderman a member of a city council

Anabaptists "radical" Protestants who believed that only adults, not babies, should be baptized. Many Anabaptists also supported nonviolence and gave women and men equal roles in religion.

apprentice a young person being trained in a craft or trade by assisting and working for a master in that craft or trade

ballad a long, rhyming poem or song that tells a story

bishop a high-ranking priest in the Catholic Church or Church of England who oversees religious affairs for a particular region

bloodletting a common Renaissance medical procedure, performed to both treat and prevent disease

bower a shelter made from tree branches, often decorated with flowers

broadside a single sheet of paper, usually of a large size and sometimes folded, printed on one or both sides. Ballads were often published as broadsides.

Burgundy during the Renaissance, a duchy (territory ruled by a duke or duchess) that included parts of northern and eastern France as well as present-day Belgium and the Netherlands

Catholic refers to the branch of Christianity under the authority of the pope

chancellor a ruler's secretary. The Lord Chancellor of England was head of the country's judicial system and presided over the House of Lords in Parliament.

congregation the group of people who attend a particular church

convent a common term for a women's monastery

courtier a person who lived at or regularly attended a ruler's court

dowry money, property, and goods supplied by a bride's family for her to bring into her marriage

excommunication action taken by the Catholic Church to deny Holy Communion and the other sacraments to a person or group of people, usually as a punishment for a serious crime against Church law; the exclusion of a person from Church membership

fallow describes land in which no seeds are planted so that it can "rest" and regain its fertility

fool a clownlike character popular in Renaissance plays and celebrations

fresco a wall painting made on fresh plaster

grammar to Renaissance humanists, the study of languages, especially ancient Greek and Latin

guild an organization of people in the same craft or trade. The guild set standards of training and workmanship and looked after its members' interests in various ways.

Holy Roman Empire an empire made up primarily of German, Austrian, and Italian territories, founded in 962 CE with the idea of unifying Europe

Huguenots French Protestants, who were followers of Jean Calvin

humanism an approach to learning that emphasized study of the subjects known as the humanities: grammar, rhetoric, literature, philosophy, and history. A humanist was someone who had thoroughly studied the humanities.

journeyman from the French word *journée*, "a day's work"; a craftsperson who has completed apprenticeship but has not yet become a master

Low Countries modern-day Belgium, Luxembourg, and the Netherlands. During much of the Renaissance they were part of the Holy Roman Empire.

manuscript in Renaissance times, a book that was written out, illustrated, and bound by hand

martyr someone who is killed because of his or her religion

mercenary a soldier who fights only for money (as opposed to fighting out of loyalty to a country or cause)

missionary a person who travels to a far-off place to teach his or her religion to the people

moat a wide, deep trench, usually filled with water, used as a defensive barrier—for example, to surround a city or castle

monastery a religious institution where monks or nuns live apart from the world, devoting themselves to prayer and study

monk a man who lives in a monastery, taking lifelong vows of poverty, chastity, and obedience

Muslim a follower of Islam, the religion founded in seventh-century Arabia by Muhammad

notary a person who wrote out legal or official documents for individuals. Like a modern notary public, a Renaissance notary could also certify documents to make them official.

nun a woman who lives in a convent, taking lifelong vows of poverty, chastity, and obedience

Ottoman Empire an empire based in Turkey, founded in the fourteenth century. At its peak in the 1500s it included North Africa, most of the Middle East, and much of southeastern Europe.

patron someone who gives financial support and other encouragement to an artist, musician, writer, etc.

penance actions undertaken to atone for, or make up for, sins

pilgrimage a journey to a holy site, such as a place associated with Jesus or a church with important saints' relics

podere in northern Italy, a plot of land owned by a landlord and worked by a share-cropper

Protestant refers to Christians who reject the authority of the pope and many practices and beliefs of the Catholic Church

Psalms a book of the Bible containing songlike poems of prayer and praise

Puritans English Protestants who followed the teachings of Jean Calvin

Reformation the movement begun in 1517 by Martin Luther to reform the Church. Eventually the Reformation resulted in the founding of many different kinds of Christian groups, such as Lutherans, Anglicans (Episcopalians), Calvinists (Presbyterians), and Baptists.

regent a person who governs a territory on behalf of the official ruler, often because the ruler is too young or too sick to exercise authority

republic a form of government in which citizens elect officials to represent them

rhetoric the art of using language to persuade through eloquent speech or writing

Roman Empire At its height, the empire stretched from Spain to the Middle East, reaching north to include what is now England and south to include North Africa. In 330 the empire's capital moved from Rome to Constantinople, and in 364 the empire was divided into eastern and western halves. The last emperor of the Western Empire was overthrown in 476, while the Eastern Empire survived, as the Byzantine Empire, for nearly a thousand years more.

rosary a string of beads, held in the hands, used by many Catholics to assist in their praying

saint a person recognized by the Catholic Church as being especially holy and able to perform miracles both during life and after death

scribe a person who copied out books or documents by hand

serf an unfree peasant, not allowed to leave the landlord's estate or to marry someone from off the estate, and owing various fees and a set amount of work to the landlord

tithe a kind of tax collected by the Church; it was supposed to be one-tenth of a household's income

FOR FURTHER READING

Ashby, Ruth. *Elizabethan England*. New York: Benchmark Books, 1999.

Claybourne, Anna. *The Renaissance*. Chicago, IL: Raintree, 2008.

Cole, Alison. *Renaissance*. London and New York: Dorling Kindersley, 2000.

Fitzpatrick, Anne. *The Renaissance: Movements in Art*. Mankato, MN: Creative Education, 2006.

Gallagher, Jim. *Sir Francis Drake and the Foundation of a World Empire*. Philadelphia: Chelsea House, 2001.

Greenblatt, Miriam. *Elizabeth I and Tudor England*. New York: Benchmark Books, 2002.

———. *Lorenzo de' Medici and Renaissance Italy*. New York: Benchmark Books, 2003.

Greenhill, Wendy. *Shakespeare's Theater*. Chicago: Heinemann Library, 2000.

Halliwell, Sarah, ed. *The Renaissance: Artists and Writers*. Austin: Raintree Steck-Vaughn, 1998.

Hinds, Kathryn. *Life in Elizabethan England: The Church*. New York: Benchmark Books, 2008.

———. *Life in Elizabethan England: The City*. New York: Benchmark Books, 2008.

———. *Life in Elizabethan England: The Countryside*. New York: Benchmark Books, 2008.

———. *Life in Elizabethan England: The Court*. New York: Benchmark Books, 2008.

———. *Venice and Its Merchant Empire*. New York: Benchmark Books, 2001.

Lassieur, Allison. *Leonardo da Vinci and the Renaissance in World History*. Berkeley Heights, NJ: Enslow Publishers, 2000.

Mann, Kenny. *Isabel, Ferdinand, and Fifteenth-Century Spain*. New York: Benchmark Books, 2002.

Mason, Antony. *Everyday Life in the Renaissance*. North Mankato, MN: Smart Apple Media, 2005.

Matthews, Rupert. *The Renaissance*. New York: Peter Bedrick, 2000.

Merlo, Claudio. *Three Masters of the Renaissance: Leonardo, Michelangelo, Raphael.* Translated by Marion Lignana Rosenberg. Hauppauge, NY: Barron's Educational Series, 1999.

Millar, Heather. *Spain in the Age of Exploration.* New York: Benchmark Books, 1999.

Mühlberger, Richard. *What Makes a Bruegel a Bruegel?* New York: Metropolitan Museum of Art/Viking, 1993.

———. *What Makes a Leonardo a Leonardo?* New York: Metropolitan Museum of Art/Viking, 1994.

Netzley, Patricia D. *Life During the Renaissance.* San Diego: Lucent Books, 1998.

Pollard, Michael. *Johann Gutenberg: Master of Modern Printing.* Woodbridge, CT: Blackbirch Press, 2001.

Rosen, Michael. *Shakespeare: His Work and His World.* Cambridge, MA: Candlewick Press, 2001.

Ruggiero, Adriane. *The Ottoman Empire.* New York: Benchmark Books, 2003.

Schomp, Virginia. *The Italian Renaissance.* New York: Benchmark Books, 2003.

Thomas, Jane Resh. *Behind the Mask: The Life of Queen Elizabeth I.* New York: Clarion Books, 1998.

Thomson, Melissa, and Ruth Dean. *Women of the Renaissance.* San Diego, CA: Lucent Books, 2005.

Ventura, Piero. *Michelangelo's World.* New York: Putnam, 1989.

Wood, Tim. *The Renaissance.* New York: Viking, 1993.

Yancey, Diane. *Life in the Elizabethan Theater.* San Diego: Lucent Books, 1997.

ONLINE INFORMATION

Annenberg Media. *Renaissance.*
> http://www.learner.org/interactives/renaissance

The Artchive: Renaissance Art.
> http://artchive.com/artchive/renaissance.html

Chiarini, Gloria. *The Florence Art Guide.*
> http://www.mega.it/eng/egui/hogui.htm

Johnson, Phil. *The Hall of Church History: The Reformers.*
> http://www.spurgeon.org/~phil/rformers.htm

Jokinen, Anniina. *16th Century Renaissance English Literature (1485–1603).*
> http://www.luminarium.org/renlit

A Journey through the Renaissance.
> http://library.thinkquest.org/C005356/index2.htm

Kren, Emil, and Daniel Marx. *Web Gallery of Art.*
> http://www.wga.hu

Matthews, Kevin, and Artifice, Inc. *Renaissance Architecture.*
> http://www.greatbuildings.com/types/styles/renaissance.html

Secara, Maggie. *Life in Elizabethan England: A Compendium of Common Knowledge.*
> http://elizabethan.org/compendium/home.html

Shakespeare Resource Center.
> http://www.bardweb.net

Sites on Shakespeare and the Renaissance.
> http://internetshakespeare.uvic.ca/Annex/links/index.html

Vatican Exhibit.
> http://www.ibiblio.org/expo/vatican.exhibit/Vatican.exhibit.html

SELECTED BIBLIOGRAPHY

Allison, Alexander W., et al., eds. *The Norton Anthology of Poetry*. Rev. ed. New York: Norton, 1975.

Barber, C. L. *Shakespeare's Festive Comedy: A Study of Dramatic Form and Its Relation to Social Custom*. Princeton, NJ: Princeton University Press, 1959.

Bell, Rudolph M. *How to Do It: Guides to Good Living for Renaissance Italians*. Chicago and London: University of Chicago Press, 1999.

Black, C. F., et al. *Cultural Atlas of the Renaissance*. New York: Prentice Hall General Reference, 1993.

Braudel, Fernand. *Civilization and Capitalism, 15th–18th Century*. Translated by Siân Reynolds. 3 vols. New York: Harper and Row, 1982.

Bristol, Michael D. *Carnival and Theater: Plebeian Culture and the Structure of Authority in Renaissance England*. New York and London: Routledge, 1985.

Brown, Howard M. *Music in the Renaissance*. Englewood Cliffs, NJ: Prentice Hall, 1976.

Brown, Patricia Fortini. *Art and Life in Renaissance Venice*. New York: Harry N. Abrams, 1997.

Brucker, Gene. *Renaissance Florence*. New York: John Wiley, 1969.

Campion, Thomas. *The Works of Thomas Campion*. Edited by Walter R. Davis. New York: Norton, 1970.

Caselli, Giovanni. *The Renaissance and the New World*. New York: Peter Bedrick, 1985.

Chojnacka, Monica. *Working Women of Early Modern Venice*. Baltimore and London: Johns Hopkins University Press, 2001.

Darnton, Robert. "Peasants Tell Tales: The Meaning of Mother Goose" in *The Great Cat Massacre and Other Episodes in French Cultural History*. New York: Basic Books, 1984.

Davis, Michael Justin. *The England of William Shakespeare*. New York: Dutton, 1987.

Davis, Natalie Zemon. *The Return of Martin Guerre*. Cambridge, MA: Harvard University Press, 1983.

———. *Society and Culture in Early Modern France*. Stanford, CA: Stanford University Press, 1975.

Denieul-Cormier, Annie. *The Renaissance in France, 1488–1559*. Translated by Anne and Christopher Fremantle. London: George Allen and Unwin, 1968.

Douglass, Jane Dempsey. "Women and the Continental Reformation" in *Religion and Sexism: Images of Woman in the Jewish and Christian Traditions*. Edited by Rosemary Radford Ruether. New York: Simon and Schuster, 1974.

Durant, Will. *The Reformation: A History of European Civilization from Wyclif to Calvin: 1300–1564*. Vol. VI, *The Story of Civilization*. New York: Simon and Schuster, 1957.

Editors of Time-Life Books. *What Life Was Like in the Realm of Elizabeth: England AD 1533–1603*. Alexandria, VA: Time-Life Books, 1998.

———. *What Life Was Like at the Rebirth of Genius: Renaissance Italy, AD 1400–1550*. Alexandria, VA: Time-Life Books, 1999.

Ferguson, Sinclair B., and David F. Wright, eds. *New Dictionary of Theology*. Downers Grove, IL: InterVarsity Press, 1988.

Gilbert, Sandra M., and Susan Gubar. *The Norton Anthology of Literature by Women: The Tradition in English*. New York: Norton, 1985.

Ginzburg, Carlo. *The Night Battles: Witchcraft and Agrarian Cults in the Sixteenth and Seventeenth Centuries*. Translated by John and Anne Tedeschi. New York: Penguin Books, 1985.

Grendler, Paul F., ed. in chief. *Encyclopedia of the Renaissance*. 6 vols. New York: Charles Scribner's Sons, 1999.

Hale, John. *The Civilization of Europe in the Renaissance*. New York: Touchstone, 1993.

Hoffman, Philip T. *Growth in a Traditional Society: The French Countryside, 1450–1815*. Princeton, NJ: Princeton University Press, 1996.

Hoffmeister, Gerhart, ed. *The Renaissance and Reformation in Germany: An Introduction*. New York: Frederick Ungar Publishing, 1977.

Huse, Norbert, and Wolfgang Wolters. *The Art of Renaissance Venice: Architecture, Sculpture, and Painting, 1460–1590*. Translated by Edmund Jephcott. Chicago and London: University of Chicago Press, 1990.

Jardine, Lisa. *Worldly Goods: A New History of the Renaissance*. New York: Doubleday, 1996.

Jardine, Lisa, and Jerry Brotton. *Global Interests: Renaissance Art between East and West*. Ithaca: Cornell University Press, 2000.

Johnson, Paul. *The Renaissance: A Short History*. New York: Modern Library, 2000.

Kekewich, Lucille, ed. *The Impact of Humanism*. New Haven and London: Yale University Press, 2000.

Kelsey, Harry. *Sir Francis Drake: The Queen's Pirate*. New Haven and London: Yale University Press, 1998.

King, Margaret L. *Women of the Renaissance*. Chicago and London: University of Chicago Press, 1991.

King, Ross. *Brunelleschi's Dome: How a Renaissance Genius Reinvented Architecture*. New York: Walker, 2000.

Kurlansky, Mark. *Cod: A Biography of the Fish That Changed the World*. New York: Penguin Books, 1997.

Liebowitz, Ruth P. "Virgins in the Service of Christ: The Dispute over an Active Apostolate for Women during the Counter-Reformation" in *Women of Spirit: Female Leadership in the Jewish and Christian Traditions*. Edited by Rosemary Ruether and Eleanor McLaughlin. New York: Simon and Schuster, 1979.

Logan, George M., et al., eds. *The Norton Anthology of English Literature*. 7th ed. Volume 1B, *The Sixteenth Century, The Early Seventeenth Century*. New York: Norton, 2000.

Mateer, David, ed. *Courts, Poets, and Patrons*. New Haven and London: Yale University Press, 2000.

Mazzanti, Anna. *The Art of Florence in Its Great Museums*. Translated by Christopher Evans. Florence: Scala, 1997.

Merlo, Claudio. *Three Masters of the Renaissance: Leonardo, Michelangelo, Raphael*. Translated by Marion Lignana Rosenberg. Hauppauge, NY: Barron's Educational Series, 1999.

Metford, J. C. J. *Dictionary of Christian Lore and Legend*. London: Thames and Hudson, 1983.

Mitchell, Bonner. *Rome in the High Renaissance: The Age of Leo X*. Norman, OK: University of Oklahoma Press, 1973.

Monter, E. William. *Calvin's Geneva*. New York: John Wiley, 1967.

Mottola, Anthony, trans. *The Spiritual Exercises of St. Ignatius*. Garden City, NY: Image Books, 1964.

Murray, John J. *Antwerp in the Age of Plantin and Brueghel*. Norman, OK: University of Oklahoma Press, 1970.

Pritchard, R. E., ed. *Shakespeare's England: Life in Elizabethan and Jacobean Times.* Gloucestershire, England: Sutton Publishing, 1999.

Rabb, Theodore. *Renaissance Lives: Portraits of an Age.* New York: Pantheon, 1993.

Reader's Digest Association. *Everyday Life through the Ages.* London and New York: Reader's Digest Association, 1992.

Roberts, J. M. *The Making of the European Age.* New York: Oxford University Press, 1999.

Rowse, A. L. *The Elizabethan Renaissance: The Life of the Society.* New York: Charles Scribner's Sons, 1971.

Shakespeare, William. *Complete Works.* Compact ed. Edited by Stanley Wells et al. Oxford, England: Clarendon Press, 1988.

Singman, Jeffrey L. *Daily Life in Elizabethan England.* Westport, CT: Greenwood Press, 1995.

Strauss, Gerald. *Nuremberg in the Sixteenth Century.* New York: John Wiley, 1966.

Tannahill, Reay. *Food in History.* New York: Stein and Day, 1973.

Wheaton, Barbara Ketcham. *Savoring the Past: The French Kitchen and Table from 1300 to 1789.* New York: Touchstone, 1996.

SOURCES FOR QUOTATIONS

All Shakespeare quotes are from William Shakespeare, *Complete Works*, compact ed., edited by Stanley Wells et al. (Oxford, England: Clarendon Press, 1988). All biblical quotes are from the Revised Standard Version of the Bible.

The Court Quote on p. 24 ("more like a city") from Hale, p. 83. Quote on p. 24 ("a palace that throws") from Editors of Time-Life Books, *What Life Was Like at the Rebirth of Genius*, p. 73. Quote on p. 24 ("not left out") from Editors of Time-Life Books, *What Life Was Like at the Rebirth of Genius*, p. 72. Description of Sforza court on pp. 26–27 adapted from Mateer, p. 31. Quote on p. 39 ("to purchase favor") from Rowse, p. 63. Poem on pp. 40–41 ("Green groweth the holly") slightly adapted from Allison, p. 77. Elizabeth's speech on p. 49 from Gilbert and Gubar, p. 30. Quote on pp. 50–51 ("you will find") from King, *Women of the Renaissance*, p. 188. Quote on p. 65 ("Local and national dishes") from Kekewich, pp. 30–31.

The City Quote on p. 83 ("No other town") from Murray, pp. 3–4. Quote on p. 85 ("In this city") from Murray, p. 67. Thomas Platter's description of Paris on pp. 90–91 from Denieul-Cormier, pp. 17–19. Quote on p. 92 ("In every street") by Thomas Dekker, from Pritchard, p. 156. Poem on p. 94 ("Come to the bath house") from Strauss, p. 194. Pie recipe on pp. 104–105 adapted from Singman, p. 146. Quote on p. 107 ("For the service") from Murray, p. 67. Quote on p. 118 ("Now all disciplines") from Denieul-Cormier, p. 240. French master's description of printing on p. 123 from Denieul-Cormier, pp. 166–167. Pietro Aretino's letter on p. 126 from Rabb, p. 39. Quote on p. 132 ("Force and scare tactics") by Michele Savonarola, from Bell, pp. 154–155. Quote on p. 136 ("both have the name") from King, *Women of the Renaissance*, p. 207. Quote on p. 139 ("The women, too") from Hale, p. 507. Quote on p. 139 ("One can see") by Francesco Guicciardini, from Murray, p. 142. Dürer's description of a procession on pp. 142–143 from Murray, pp. 25–27. Quote on p. 147 ("Not a statue") from Hale, p. 460.

The Countryside Quote on p. 157 ("This Peasant Court") by Christoph Scheurl, from Strauss, p. 66. Poem on p. 167 ("Sheep have eat up") by Thomas Bustard, from Pritchard, p. 70. William Harrison's comments on bedding on p. 177 from Pritchard, pp. 52–53. Quote on pp. 184–185 ("In the orchard") from Denieul-Cormier, p. 148. Quote on p. 190 ("a poor man") from Pritchard, p. 53. Thomas Platter's description of goat herding on p. 203 from Rabb, p. 77. Poem on pp. 206–207 ("Jack and Joan") from Campion, p. 80 (spelling and capitalization modernized). Description of Barley Break on p. 211 adapted from Singman, p. 161. Quote on p. 212 ("And when they were") from Denieul-Cormier, pp. 158–159. Quote on pp. 213, 216 ("They have twenty") by Phillip Stubbes, from Barber, pp. 21–22. Noël du Fail's description of a village gathering on pp. 214–215 from Denieul-Cormier, pp. 156–157. Quote on p. 217 ("Oh, 'tis the merry time") by Nicholas Breton, from Pritchard, p. 82.

The Church Quote on p. 250 ("I must . . . acknowledge") from Mitchell, p. 107. Quote on p. 260 ("the chief mischief") from Rowse, p. 248. Quote on p. 262 ("like men possessed") from Durant, pp. 410, 411. Quote on p. 263 ("There are no organs") by Bernardino Ochino, from Durant, p. 476. Description of corrupt monks on p. 268 by Johannes Trithemius, from Durant, p. 20. Arcangela Tarabotti's comments on unwilling nuns on pp. 276–277 from King, *Women of the Renaissance*, p. 90. Quote on p. 278 ("The wives") from King, *Women of the Renaissance*, pp. 99–100. Quotes on p. 281 ("I saw Him" and "In his hands") from Rabb, pp. 101, 103. Quote on p. 282 ("The greatest gift") from Durant, p. 417. Quote on p. 282 ("If a mother") from Douglass, p. 295. Katherine Zell's letter on p. 283 from King, *Women of the Renaissance*, p. 137. Recipe for hot cross buns on p. 288 based on recipes from Irma S. Rombauer and Marion Rombauer Becker, *The Joy of Cooking* (Indianapolis, IN: Bobbs-Merrill, 1975). Quote on p. 290 ("Any exercise") by Philip Stubbes, from Rowse, p. 221. Description of a devout villager on p. 292 from Ginzburg, p. 120. Quote on p. 294 ("I . . . take thee") from Logan, p. 555. Quote on p. 298 ("The Spanish Fleet") by John Gerard, from Editors of Time-Life Books, *What Life Was Like in the Realm of Elizabeth*, pp. 103–104. Quote on p. 301 ("They who at first") by Hendrik Spieghel, from Murray, p. 41. Quotes on p. 302 ("the true school" and "all the evils") from Black, p. 179.

INDEX

Page numbers for illustrations are in boldface

PICTURE CREDITS

Images provided by Rose Corbett Gordon, Art Editor of Mystic CT, from the following sources:

Front cover: Collection of the Earl of Leicester, Holkham Hall, Norfolk/ Bridgeman Art Library.

Back cover: Erich Lessing/Art Resource, NY.

Page 1: Johnny van Haeften Gallery, London/Bridgeman Art Library; page 4: Bridgeman Art Library/Getty Images; page 5: The Art Archive/Musée du Louvre Paris/Alfredo Dagli Orti; page 6: Corsham Court, Wiltshire/Bridgeman Art Library.

The Court Page 8, 38, 62: Erich Lessing/Art Resource, NY; page 10: Alinari/Art Resource, NY; page 13: Museo Real Academia de Bellas Artes, Madrid/Bridgeman Art Library; page 15: National Gallery, London/ Bridgeman Art Library; page 16: Pelworth House, Sussex/Art Resource, NY; page 19: Giraudon/Art Resource, NY; page 20: Staatliche Museen Kassel; page 22: Museo di Firenze Com'era, Florence/Bridgeman Art Library; page 23: Palazzo Ducale, Mantua/Bridgeman Art Library; page 27: J. Paul Getty Museum, Los Angeles/Bridgeman Art Library; page 28: National Portrait Gallery, London/Bridgeman Art Library; page 30: Hermitage, St. Petersburg/Bridgeman Art Library; page 34: Czartoryski Museum, Krakow/ Bridgeman Art Library; page 41: Burghley House Collection, Lincolnshire/ Bridgeman Art Library; page 44, 51: Kunsthistorisches Museum, Vienna/ Bridgeman Art Library; page 47: Church of the Assumption Duomo Prato/ Bridgeman Art Library; page 53: Private Collection/Bridgeman Art Library; page 55: Alinari / Art Resource, NY; page 57: Scala/Art Resource, NY; page 60: Musée des Beaux-Arts, Lille/Bridgeman Art Library; page 67: Fogg Art Museum, Harvard University Art Museums/Bridgeman Art Library; page

68: Art Resource, NY; pages 70, 72: British Library/Bridgeman Art Library; page 71: British Library.

The City Page 75: Réunion des Musées Nationaux/Art Resource, NY; page 77: Palazzo Vecchio (Palazzo della Signoria) Florence/Bridgeman Art Library; page 81: Stapleton Collection, UK/Bridgeman Art Library; pages 82, 89, 117: Private Collection/Bridgeman Art Library; page 84: Hamburg Kunsthalle, Hamburg/Bridgeman Art Library; pages 87, 96: Museo de Firenze Com'era, Florence/Bridgeman Art Library; pages 92, 126, 128, 140: Erich Lessing/Art Resource, NY; pages 99, 102, 106, 148, 151; Scala/Art Resource, NY; page 100: Waterman Fine Art Ltd., London/Bridgeman Art Library; page 108: Castello di Issogne, Val d'Aosta, Italy/Bridgeman Art Library; page 109: Musée National de la Renaissance, Ecouen, France/ Giraudon-Bridgeman Art Library; page 112: Museo Civico, Bologna/ Giraudon-Bridgeman Art Library; page 115: British Library/ Bridgeman Art Library; pages 121, 135: Victoria & Albert Museum/Art Resource, NY; page 123: Giraudon/Art Resource, NY; page 132: Kunsthistorisches Museum, Vienna/Ali Meyer/Bridgeman Art Library; page 143: Victoria & Albert Museum/Bridgeman Art Library; page 144: Hermitage, St. Petersburg/Peter Willi/Bridgeman Art Library.

The Country Page 153: Bibliothèque de l'Arsenal/Archives Charmet/ Bridgeman Art Library; pages 155, 163, 166, 171, 173: Scala/Art Resource, NY; pages 157, 168, 184, 185, 195, 211: The Pierpont Morgan Library/Art Resource, NY; pages 159, 191, 221: Réunion des Musées Nationaux/Art Resource, NY; page 175: The Barnes Foundation, Merion, Pennsylvania/ Bridgeman Art Library; page 177: Art Resource, NY; pages 182, 193: Alinari/ Art Resource, NY; page 188: By Courtesy of the National Portrait Gallery, London; pages 197, 210, 215: Erich Lessing/Art Resource, NY; page 200: Louvre, Paris/Giraudon-Bridgeman Art Library; page 202: Offentliche Kunstsammlung, Basel, Switzerland/Giraudon-Bridgeman Art Library; page 204: Johnny van Haeften Gallery, London/Bridgeman Art Library; page 206: Fine Arts Photographic Library, London/Art Resource, NY; page 216: Fitzwilliam Museum, University of Cambridge, UK/Bridgeman Art Library; page 219: British Library, London/Bridgeman Art Library; page 223: Private Collection/Bridgeman Art Library; page 224: Foto Marburg/Art Resource, NY.

The Church Page 227: Peter Willi/Bridgeman Art Library; pages 229, 258: Museo di San Marco dell'Angelico, Florence/Bridgeman Art Library; page 231: Museo Poldi Pezzoli. Milan/Bridgeman Art Library; page 233: The Art Archive/Musée Royale des Beaux-Arts Antwerp/Album/Joseph Marti; page 235: Ognissanti Church, Florence/Bridgeman Art Library; page 236: Alinari/Art Resource, NY; page 237, 274: Private Collection/Bridgeman Art Library; pages 238, 261, 277, 287: Art Resource, NY; page 240: Palazzo Ducale, Urbino/Bridgeman Art Library; page 243: Vatican Museums and Galleries/Bridgeman Art Library; page 244: National Gallery, London/ Bridgeman Art Library; page 245: Index/Bridgeman Art Library; page 247: The Art Archive/Palatine Library Parma/Dagli Orti; page 249: Pierpont Morgan Library/Art Resource, NY; page 251: Germanisches Nationalmuseum, Nuremberg/Bridgeman Art Library; page 253: Museo Nazionale di Capodimonte, Naples/Art Resource, NY; page 257: The Art Archive/Dagli Orti; page 263: The Art Archive/University Library Geneva/Dagli Orti; page 265: The Art Archive/Archaeological Museum Madrid/Dagli Orti; page 267: Monte Oliveto Maggiore, Tuscany/Bridgeman Art Library; page 269: The Art Archive/Santa Maria della Scala Hospital Siena/Dagli Orti (A); page 271: Kunsthistorisches Museum, Vienna/Bridgeman Art Library; page 279: The Berger Collection at the Denver Art Museum/ Bridgeman Art Library; page 281, 285: Corbis; page 291: Bibliothèque de l'Histoire du Protestantisme, Giraudon/Bridgeman Art Library; page 293: The Art Archive/Museo del Prado Madrid/Dagli Orti; page 297: The Stapleton Collection/Bridgeman Art Library; page 300: The Art Archive/ Musée du Louvre Paris/Dagli Orti; page 303: Giraudon/ Bridgeman Art Library.

ABOUT THE AUTHOR

Kathryn Hinds grew up near Rochester, New York. She studied music and writing at Barnard College, and did graduate work in comparative literature and medieval studies at the City University of New York. She has written more than forty books for young people, most recently the four-volume series LIFE IN THE MEDIEVAL MUS-LIM WORLD. Kathryn lives in the north Georgia mountains with her husband, their son, and an assortment of cats and dogs. When she is not reading or writing, she enjoys music, dancing, gardening, knitting, and taking walks in the woods. Visit Kathryn online at http://www.kathrynhinds.com